WAYNE ROONEY

WAYNE ROONEY
My Story So Far

Wayne Rooney
with Hunter Davies

HarperSport

An Imprint of HarperCollins*Publishers*

First published in the UK in 2006 by
HarperSport
an imprint of HarperCollins*Publishers*
London

© Wayne Rooney 2006

1

A CIP catalogue record for this book
is available from the British Library

ISBN-13 978-0-00-723628-2
ISBN-10 0-00-723628-X

All plate section photographs provided courtesy
of Wayne Rooney with the exception of the following:
Action Images 12, 13, 14, 15, 18, 19, 21, 22 (top left and centre),
23, 24; **Mercury Press** 5 (centre), 10, 11, 16 (bottom),
20 (right and bottom)

Set in Sabon by
Rowland Phototypesetting Ltd,
Bury St Edmunds, Suffolk

Printed and bound in Great Britain by
Clays Ltd, St Ives plc

The HarperCollins website address is
www.harpercollins.co.uk

Contents

'We have got the best young player this country has seen in the past 30 years.'
Sir Alex Ferguson

'He is not a potential talent anymore, he is ready. I don't need to tell him how to score goals – his vision is incredible, he's ready for anything.'
Sven-Goran Eriksson

'He's a very exciting talent who shows maturity and composure beyond his young years.'
Pelé

'Wayne Rooney is a phenomenal talent and has already achieved a lot. He could go on to be as great as Bobby Charlton and help England win the World Cup.'
Diego Maradona

'Rooney's one of the best players in the world, without doubt.'
Ronaldinho

Acknowledgements

Thanks and thanks again to my Mum and Dad for, well being my mum and dad, having me, caring for me and helping me in those early years when we didn't know where things would lead.

To Coleen for her constant love, support and encouragement, and to her parents and family for their help plus all the meals.

To all the coaches who've had an influence on my career, and to friends and extended family for always being there.

To Paul Stretford for his wisdom and advice, and to all the Proactive team.

To the HarperCollins editorial team for pulling it all together.

Finally, thanks to Hunter Davies for dragging it all out of me. Well played, Hunter.

Introduction

Stamford Bridge, 29 April 2006. Chelsea got an early goal. William Gallas headed in from a corner, which of course should never have happened after all the work we do in training defending set-pieces. Five minutes in and we were already chasing the game.

All the same, in the first half, we didn't do too badly. I had a chance when I broke away down the middle, got into the penalty area, managed to hold off two defenders, with only the goalie to beat – but I shot wide. Some commentators later said the grass was too long that day. I'm not blaming the grass. The ball just got stuck under my foot and I didn't manage a clear shot.

In the second half, we went two-down when Joe Cole scored. Then I got booked for a rash tackle and the crowd started shouting, '*Rooney, Rooney, what's the score?*' In the 72nd minute, they scored a third. I felt sick. It was horrible. I could sense some of our team wanting it to be all over, just waiting for the whistle to blow, though I don't think our heads went down. Mine certainly didn't. It never does. However late in the game, however desperate, I always think I'll score.

In the 78th minute, I got another chance. This time to the left, heading towards the Chelsea penalty area. As I was breaking away, their full-back, Paulo Ferreira, caught me. It was a fair tackle, nothing nasty, but he managed to nick the ball off me. More of a tangle rather than a tackle, really. I went down. And I stayed down.

Somehow, his knee had banged into the back of my right calf. The impact made my lower leg buckle under the pressure. Immediately, I felt something pop. In my right foot. But I didn't know where or what.

All I knew was that the pain was agonising.

I couldn't move and was almost in tears, holding my head with the pain. Play stopped, as everyone began to realise I'd suffered some sort of serious injury. The physios and the stretcher-bearers ran on. The crowd was hushed.

As I was carried off the pitch, I could hear the Chelsea fans, who had been jeering me when I'd been yellow-carded, slowly clapping me off. I remember thinking, 'They don't need to do that – but nice of them, all the same.'

In the dressing room, the United doctor, Doc Stone, checked me out, trying to work out what I'd done. I was confused because it felt different from the last time I'd damaged my foot, in Euro 2004. On that occasion, I hadn't heard any pop, and didn't feel pain until I put my boot back on.

The doc's first thought was that I'd just overstretched the nerves. There'd been no serious tackle, I'd not been clattered. But I thought no, it's more than that. Something has gone. I heard it.

The doc said if it was overstretched nerves, I'd be out for two weeks. I thought, oh no, I'll miss our last two games of the season.

Then I thought, if something has really gone wrong, if it's a broken metatarsal, like that last time, I could miss the World Cup.

In the dressing room, it was very quiet. Not really because of me but because of our performance, being stuffed by Chelsea. No one was talking. The Boss didn't lay into us. He didn't have to. We all knew we'd played rubbish.

It was decided I would go back to Manchester with the team rather than to a London hospital for an X-ray.

There was dead silence on the train. We were all so gutted. I didn't have the energy to play cards. I didn't even play my music.

Last time, it had been fourteen weeks before I'd played again. I was working it out in my head. The Chelsea game was Saturday, 29 April. England's first World Game game against Paraguay was Saturday 10 June. That meant it was exactly six weeks ahead.

If my injury was anywhere near as serious as I felt it was, I had no chance.

I'd left my car at Old Trafford. The players always do that, before any match, home or away. I couldn't drive it of course. My foot was all strapped up with ice packs and stuff, but the pain had subsided, as I'd been given painkillers.

Fortunately, that day Wes Brown had come in with me to Old Trafford. He lives quite near me, so I'd given him a lift in my car. He said he would take it home for me.

From Manchester Piccadilly I went with the club doctor straight to the BUPA hospital in Whalley Range, where I had an X-ray. It showed nothing. But that didn't reassure me. I knew what I'd heard and felt. They then did a scan, a CT scan, I think it's called. That went on for a long time, some 45 minutes, with them asking me to hold on, while they did more. I realised by then that they had seen something.

Finally I was told the horrific news – I had fractured the fourth metatarsal in my right foot – and also chipped the third metatarsal. There was more damage than even I'd imagined.

I had by then begun to think that perhaps I had imagined the pop. Or just hoped I had. Now I was devastated. It was the worst single moment in my life so far.

Things were repeating themselves. Euro 2004, my first big tournament, had ended for me when I'd suffered the same injury. And in a clash with a Portuguese player.

It was by now ten o'clock at night. I had rang Coleen

4

earlier, but I knew she would be waiting for my call. I only said a few words on the phone. I'd see her soon, she had been at a birthday party with her mates earlier in the day and was waiting at her mum's in Liverpool. I wasn't sure who was going to take me home from the hospital, or whether I wanted to go home.

All these last ten years, all that hard work, all the dreams, playing football in the street and imagining I was Michael Owen. All that effort and sacrifice. It wasn't luck, getting to this stage. I deserved it. Now it looked as if my World Cup would be over before it had even begun . . .

ONE

Family Fun

I was nearly called Adrian. That was what my father wanted. A bit posh, I suppose, and doesn't quite sound like me. I wonder if I would have had a different personality if I'd gone through life with a different name? In the end, though, my mum talked my dad out of it.

His idea was to name me after Adrian Heath, one of the Everton stars, a little bloke, very quick and clever, who later went into coaching with Peter Reid, then manager at Sunderland. I was a big fan of his, but I don't think I would have fancied having the name Adrian.

So I was christened Wayne – after my dad. My mum insisted as she felt the first-born son should be named after the father. That was a tradition in her family.

The Rooney family, I suppose, must have come from Ireland, but I've no idea when or from where. It could well have been some time ago, because none of my relations in living memory came from the Emerald Isle.

Someone is working on the family tree at the moment, so I'll let you know if they find anything of interest.

It wasn't in fact until I got to secondary school that I was aware I was probably of Irish descent. One of the teachers, when she was looking down the list of all the new boys, was commenting on the different surnames: 'You must be from a Scottish family, you must have some Welsh blood, you, Rooney, are obviously Irish . . .'

I came home and said to my dad: 'Are we Irish?' 'How do I know?' he replied. My dad has always been fairly laid back.

Within the family, he is always known as 'Big Wayne' while I am 'Little Wayne'. It annoyed me when I got to about 14, and shot up and became bigger than him – he's only five feet six, two inches smaller than my mum, so it wasn't hard. But they still insisted I was Little Wayne and he was Big Wayne.

My dad was born on 1 June 1963, in Croxteth in Liverpool. His father, who worked for the Council as a labourer, had been born in Bootle but that's all I know. We called him Rick, so I suppose he must have been christened Richard, and he died when I was about ten. I don't know anything about his father, my great-grandfather, or where he came from. People in our family have never been very much interested in family trees.

My dad is one of eight children. He had four brothers and three sisters. They were all Roman Catholic, but not strict, and not regular church-goers, no more than we are.

He went to Croxteth Comprehensive School, and left at 16, without passing any exams. He became a butcher's boy for two years, until the shop closed, and later he worked in a youth club for a while before becoming a general labourer, mainly on building sites. He was often out of work so we didn't have a lot of money coming in when I was growing up. I didn't think I was missing out on anything, although we didn't have a car when I was very young. When we eventually did, they were always old bangers.

Dad was a great boxer. It ran in his family. Many of the Rooney clan were keen fighters and one of them ran a boxing club called St Theresa's. My dad weighed about ten stones in his boxing days – I won't tell you how much he weighs now or he'll thump me – but he boxed as a lightweight competing for Liverpool and then the North West Counties.

There's a photo of him being presented with a cup when he won a match against the Navy, boxing for the NW Counties. He also fought in a competition in Finland and won both gold and silver medals. His brothers Ritchie, John, Eugene and Alan won boxing cups as well, and for football, but I think my dad was the best of all of them and could have turned pro-fessional, so he says. There were people talking about it to him, but he couldn't be bothered. I don't think he fancied all the training and commitment it would have taken.

My mother was born Jeanette Morrey on 14 March 1967. Her family name is not of Irish descent but French, so they believe, but it goes back a long way and no-one knows its history. She was one of nine children – six boys and three girls – and they lived just a mile away from my dad's family, on the same council estate in Croxteth. Like my dad's family, they were Roman Catholic, but not what you would call strong church-goers. And, like my family, they were Everton fanatics. On derby day, when Everton were playing Liverpool, they would decorate the front of their house with blue and white banners and posters.

My mother's dad, William Morrey, was a labourer, working for the Metal Box Company. At one time he'd been a semi-professional footballer with Southport. Mums brothers were also keen sportsmen. Her older brother, Billie, played for Marine, a good non-league club from Crosby, and later went out to Australia to play as a semi-professional for Green Gully in Mel-bourne. He stayed on when he stopped playing and is still living Down Under.

Another brother, Vincent, got a schoolboy Under-15 cap for England, although just the one. When the Morreys decorated their house in Everton colours for big games, the brothers would also display all their cups and medals in the front window.

My mum was good at sports. She was keen on running, netball and rounders, and represented her school. She was asked to enter for national trials, so she always used to tell me, but she never did – couldn't be bothered, I suppose.

She left school at 16, with no certificates, but got on a Youth Training scheme, and went on a year's course to learn typing. She had hoped to get a job in an office, but none came up and so she was out of work.

She met my dad not long afterwards, when she was about 17 and he about 20. He was still a keen boxer at the time and used to go on training runs round our estate. Most evenings he would run past her house in Storrington Avenue, although he jokes now that he never ran fast enough. Anyway, they got talking one evening, and he asked her out. And that was that.

After about six months of going out together, mum fell pregnant. It was a big shock because she'd led herself to believe she could never have a baby. When she was aged about six she suffered very serious hepatitis and was in hospital for over three months with an infection of the liver and kidneys. This was why she believed that she would never conceive. So when she told her mum she was pregnant it came as a bit of a surprise. They were both delighted, and my grandmother went straight to church to pray that she would be okay.

They were each living in their own family homes, my mum and my dad, until my mum was seven months'

QBDX 569779			

Application Number... G289391

CERTIFIED COPY   **OF AN ENTRY**

NHS Number	**YGLWE III**	**BIRTH**	Entry No. **III**

Registration district	*Liverpool*	Administrative area
Sub-district	*Fazakerley Metropolitan District of Liverpool*	

CHILD

1. Date and place of birth   *Twenty Fourth October, 1985 Fazakerley Hospital Fazakerley*

2. Name and surname	*Wayne Mark* ROONEY	3. Sex *Male*

FATHER

4. Name and surname   *Thomas Wayne* ROONEY

5. Place of birth   *Everton, Liverpool*

6. Occupation   *Youth and Community Worker*

MOTHER

7. Name and surname   *Jeanette Marie* MORREY

8. Place of birth   *Liverpool*

9.(a) Maiden surname   ———   (b) Surname at marriage if different from maiden surname   ———

10. Usual address (if different from place of child's birth)   *38, Storrington Avenue, Liverpool, II.*

INFORMANT

11. Name and surname (if not the mother or father)	12. Qualification *Father Mother*

13. Usual address (if different from that in 10 above)   *39, Stonebridge Lane, Liverpool, II.*   *38, Storrington Avenue, Liverpool, II.*

14. I certify that the particulars entered above are true to the best of my knowledge and belief   *T.W. Rooney*   *J.M. Morrey*   Signature of Informant

15. Date of registration	16. Signature of registrar
Eleventh November, 1985.	*June Howarth. Registrar.*

17. Name given after registration, and surname

*See notes overleaf

CERTIFIED to be a true copy of an entry in the certified copy of a register of Births or Deaths in the District above mentioned. Given at the GENERAL REGISTER OFFICE. under the Seal of the said Office on   22nd   April   2006

CAUTION: THERE ARE OFFENCES RELATING TO FALSIFYING OR ALTERING A CERTIFICATE AND USING OR POSSESSING A FALSE CERTIFICATE ©CROWN COPYRIGHT

WARNING: A CERTIFICATE IS NOT EVIDENCE OF IDENTITY.

My birth certificate.

12

pregnant. They then managed to get a one-bedroom council flat at 89 Stonebridge Lane, which was where I was born. I have no memory of it though, and it's now a drug rehabilitation centre.

I was born on 24 October 1985, at Fazakerley Hospital. I arrived three days early, apparently, and weighed 8 lb 6 oz. I was named Wayne Mark Rooney. Mark is a family name. My dad, whose job is described as youth worker on my birth certificate, was present and tells me it was a great experience. My mum says I was born with blue eyes and loads of hair which was sort of in three colours – a bit of blonde, a bit of dark and the rest mousey.

My parents didn't actually get married until seventeen months after I was born, by which time mum was pregnant again. It wasn't a church wedding. I think the priest was not keen on people getting married in church when they already had a child, and were expecting again. So it was a local register office wedding, on 21 March 1987.

They had a proper reception with a sit-down meal for about 150 guests in a room above a local pub, the Brewer's Arms. It was paid for by their mothers as my parents could not have afforded it. My mum was not working as she was already looking after one kid with another on the way. My dad, at that time, was working as a labourer, making about £120 a week, so naturally, they couldn't afford a honeymoon.

Graeme, my younger brother, was born on 15 October

1987. His full name is Graeme Andrew Sharp Rooney after Graeme Sharp, the Everton striker, whom my dad hero-worshipped. His other hero at the time was Andy Gray, another Blues legend who also played for Scotland.

I've also got a second brother, John, who was born on 17 December 1990. I think my mother would also have liked to have had a girl, but my parents stopped having children after that.

By January 1986, my mum and dad had moved from their one-bed flat to a three-bedroom council house at 28 Armill Road. We lived there for about 12 years, and it's this house I mostly remember from my childhood. The best thing about it was that at the back was a youth club, the Gems, where my dad at one time had a job. It had a five-a-side football pitch, made of tarmac, so I loved climbing over our back fence to play on it.

I started in the nursery class at Stonebridge Lane Infants School when I was about four, but have no memory of that either. My mother can clearly remember me being there – and says that on sports day I entered for every race, long and short, with and without egg and spoon, and won every one.

My mother has always been brilliantly organised and very efficient at keeping family papers and such like. In fact, she has kept every school report, certificate and official document about me and my two brothers, all filed away in plastic folders.

1992		Annual Report Key Stage 1

STONEBRIDGE LANE C.P. INFANTS

Name: **Wayne Rooney**   DOB: **24.10.85**   Year: **1**

Attendance: **A 297**
                P 310

English/Language Making progress in all areas. He will need lots of support in his reading.	**RE** Contributed to our discussions about senses nature and feelings.
Mathematics Very good in all areas. Quick to grasp new aspects. Good mental skills.	**History/Geography** We have covered aspects of these subjects during our topics - Water, Animals Homes, Ourselves and Food
Science Very keen in science to take part in discussion. Observation skills need to be encouraged.	**Creative Arts** Enjoys art and craft activities.
Technology Enjoys making things like cards, models and paper maché. Enjoyed baking and sewing.	**PE** Very keen and agile in P.E.

Personal & Social Development, Other Achievements
Wayne is popular with boys and girls of Year 1. He is a good mixer. He works hard and is rarely in trouble.

A good report, Wayne

Teacher: **W. Lee**   Headteacher: **M Rahilly**

My Stonebridge Lane Infants School report.

The first of my reports she has dates back to 1992, when I was six, from Stonebridge Lane. In English it says I needed 'lots of support' in my reading but in Maths it reads, 'quick to grasp new facts, good mental skills.' In Technology it says, 'enjoys making things like cards, models and paper maché. Enjoys baking and sewing.' God knows where all those skills have gone today. In PE I was 'very keen and agile.'

The overall report was good and comments, 'Wayne is popular with boys and girls of Year 1. He is a good mixer. He works hard and is rarely in trouble.'

My first proper memory, which still often comes into my head, happened at home when I was about five. Graeme suddenly ran out of the house into the street and I immediately ran after him, to bring him back to the house. I had no shoes on, only socks, and when I was running I scraped my foot on the floor and I hurt it so badly that the nail on my big toe came off. I got a slap, I think, from my mother, for being so clumsy and for not putting on my shoes. A pretty ordinary memory, but this is the sort of thing which seems to stick in the brain.

My mum was the one who disciplined us, with just a slap across the back of the legs, and usually because we had been playing up. I used to wind up my younger brothers, set them against each other and cause trouble, and then I'd tell my mum it was them making a noise, not me. My dad never hit me, although he was the strong figure in the background.

Family Fun

After Stonebridge Lane I moved on to Our Lady and St Swithin's, a Roman Catholic primary school in Parkstile Lane, Gillmoss, which was about a ten-minute walk from our house. We had to wear a uniform of red tie, grey jumper, grey trousers, and black shoes but no training shoes or football tops were allowed. My mother had gone to the same school, and two of her teachers, Miss Kelly and Mrs Guy also taught me. I liked Miss Kelly very much because, each day, she gave the best behaved kid a cream egg. I didn't win very often – not often enough, I thought.

For the first two weeks at St Swithin's I refused to talk to any of the boys, only to the girls. I don't know why, I just liked being with girls. Then, after about two weeks, I realised all the boys were out playing football in the playground, so I went out and joined in with them.

When I was about six, there was a girl in my class who I thought was really pretty. I once found out it was her birthday, so I bought her a box of Roses chocolates with pocket money I must have saved up or borrowed from my mother. I took the chocolates to school, and told the teacher they were for this girl's birthday.

Later on, she announced the girl's birthday to the class and asked me to come up and present the chocolates to her. I felt quite pleased and proud, but, of course, all the lads in the class gave me stick, jeering and taking the mickey: 'Is she your girlfriend, Wayne?' I immediately went red and felt really embarrassed, which I hadn't been, not until then.

There was another girl I can remember who had Down's Syndrome. She was two years older than me, and the only girl in the school we allowed to play football with the boys. She was a very strong tackler, always kicking my ankles. One day she held on to my fingers so hard I couldn't get away. I had to pull and pull, and push her away, but she still held on tightly to them. In the end I fractured one of my fingers in trying to get it free. But she was a nice girl, and I still sometimes see her and hear about her when I'm back visiting in Croxteth.

I loved St Swithin's, liked all the teachers, and I didn't cause any trouble and got good reports. In my July 1995 report, when I was nine, it says I enjoyed music, although I can't remember that now. The report adds that I became familiar with Peer Gynt. Is he the Norwegian who used to play for Manchester United?

My best subject seems to have been Religious Education: 'Wayne's recall of stories about the life of Jesus is quite detailed. His contributions to discussions show him to be a caring child who responds to the needs of others.' Oh, very true.

Next year, when I was 10, the report said I was 'quick and confident at Maths, and grasped new concepts quite quickly.' I always did like Maths.

My Physical Education report was interesting: 'Wayne can be a little boisterous at times and should learn to

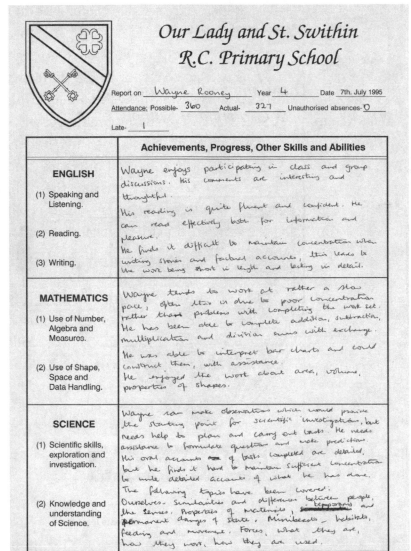

Our Lady and St. Swithin
R.C. Primary School

Report on Wayne Rooney   Year 4   Date 7th. July 1995

Attendance: Possible- 360   Actual- 327   Unauthorised absences- 0

Late- 1

	Achievements, Progress, Other Skills and Abilities
ENGLISH (1) Speaking and Listening. (2) Reading. (3) Writing.	Wayne enjoys participating in class and group discussions. His comments are interesting and thoughtful. His reading is quite fluent and confident. He can read effectively both for information and pleasure. He finds it difficult to maintain concentration when writing stories and factual accounts, this leads to the work being short in length and lacking in detail.
MATHEMATICS (1) Use of Number, Algebra and Measures. (2) Use of Shape, Space and Data Handling.	Wayne tends to work at rather a slow pace, often this is due to poor concentration rather than problems with completing the work set. He has been able to complete addition, subtraction, multiplication and division sums with exchange. He was able to interpret bar charts and could construct them, with assistance. He enjoyed the work about area, volume, properties of shapes.
SCIENCE (1) Scientific skills, exploration and investigation. (2) Knowledge and understanding of Science.	Wayne can make observations which would provide the starting point for scientific investigations, but needs help to plan and carry out tasks. He needs assistance to formulate questions and make predictions. His oral accounts of tasks completed are detailed, but he finds it hard to maintain sufficient concentration to write detailed accounts of what he has done. The following topics have been covered: Ourselves- Similarities and differences between people, the senses, Properties of materials, temporary and permanent changes of state, Minibeasts - habitats, feeding and movement, Forces, what they are, how they work, how they are used.

My Year 4 St Swithin's School report.

	Achievements, Progress, Other Skills and Abilities
RELIGIOUS EDUCATION	Wayne's recall of stories about the life of Jesus is quite detailed. His contribution to discussions show him to be a caring child, who responds to the needs of others.
TECHNOLOGY (1) Designing (2) Use of computers	Wayne's ideas for models are good, but at times he finds it hard to maintain sufficient concentration to complete his model carefully. He enjoyed having the opportunity to use the computer for word processing.
HISTORY	The topics covered were Anglo Saxons, Vikings, Ancient Egypt. Wayne's recall of the facts was good.
GEOGRAPHY	Attention focussed on world geography. The following topics were covered; identification of continents, resources, natural disasters and hazards, population, environmental issues. Very interested in environmental issues.
ART	Wayne has used a variety of media to develop his skills. He has studied the works of Lowry and Monet. He enjoyed using charcoal especially.
MUSIC	He enjoyed music making using simple instruments. Became familiar with Peer Gynt, The Planets
PHYSICAL EDUCATION	Very enthusiastic with P.E and games. Works well as a member of a team or group.
GENERAL PROGRESS - including Behaviour and Relationships.	Wayne is a popular member of the class. He has a tendency to be easily distracted from work and this affects the quality of what he does. He must develop his powers of concentration.
OTHER ACHIEVEMENTS	Plays for Coppull House Football team as centre forward. Received a trophy for being "Player of the Year". Plays snooker as a hobby.
Teacher P. J. Richards.	**Headteacher** J. A. McCall.

My Year 4 St Swithin's School report (cont'd).

control this for safety reasons.' What a cheek. I like the 'a little boisterous' reference. I wonder what made them think that?

Although I went to a Catholic primary school, as a family we didn't go to Mass very often, except on special occasions, and I remember a priest visiting the house about once a week, usually to collect money. I believed in Jesus of course, did drawings of him at school and I said my prayers most evenings. Usually, though, I was praying for Everton to win on Saturday.

I took my holy communion when I was nine. I had to wear a red sash across my chest and a red bow-tie which I hated. The minute the service was over I rushed out of the church and tore both things off.

At home, I was lucky to have my own bedroom, while Graeme and John shared, but I mostly slept in my parents' bed until I was about five. I'd got it into my head there was a yellow and green ghost in my bedroom and which I had 'seen' on the window ledge. I told some of my cousins and they agreed they had seen it as well. But I think they were just saying it to make me scared.

I eventually went back to sleeping in my own bed-room, but I always slept with the TV and the light on. I also liked the sound of the vacuum cleaner, or any other noise of a similar sort. It always seemed to get me to sleep. I would often tell my mother I was going upstairs to hoover my bedroom. She'd come up half an hour later, find the hoover still running, and me fast asleep. When my cousins found out about this habit they gave me some stick of course.

One of the little superstitions we all had, my cousins and the other kids I used to knock about with, concerned something called the Benny Bus which went round our estate. The minute you saw it you had to jump up on the nearest wall and stay there until it had passed, otherwise you got bad luck.

For a time, I used to have a phobia about never sitting in a room with the door ajar. I had to get up, close it properly, and hear it click, otherwise I wouldn't settle. It was the click, that's what I had to hear.

I've read about Gazza having similar sorts of superstitions and obsessions when he was young, but in my case they were never really serious or worrying. It never led to twitches, or any bad or funny behaviour, and my parents never seemed worried.

It was great having so many cousins, many of them being around my own age, and most living nearby. You always had someone to play with in the street. And if I was in a bad mood, was 'in a cob' as we say in Liverpool, and perhaps had rowed with my mother, I would just go round the corner to see my nan – my father's mother. She would take me in and give me sweets. Or I'd go to my Uncle Eugene's house. I knew I was his favourite and he would always spoil me.

I cried quite a bit at primary school, usually because I wanted sweets and would moan on until I got them.

We didn't eat a lot of junk food at home, and had chips perhaps once a week. It wasn't the case that we lived out of a frying pan or had burgers all the time. I was always very fond of pasta, especially with tuna, and salads. My only real weakness was sweets. I spent all my pocket money on them and often got some for free as well. My nan had a little van outside her house where she sold sweets. As I got older I'd often help her and get paid some money which I would then spend on sweets.

I was out roller-blading once with my cousin, Stephen, and I fell over and cut my knee. As I was getting up I noticed a £10 note lying in the gutter. I decided to share it with Stephen, and gave him half, while the other £5 I gave to my mum to spend at bingo.

Every year we all went to Butlins for our summer holidays. There were so many of us in the Rooney clan that we would have to hire a forty-seater coach to get us there.

One year when we came back from our week at Butlins, there had been a flood in our house. A pipe had leaked, and ruined a floor and ceiling. When my mother looked up at the ceiling she was convinced that the shape of the Cross had appeared. I think she thought it was some sort of miracle, similar to when Catholics in Portugal or Spain, or wherever, see the face of Jesus or Mary in a turnip or a slice of bread. She ran off to tell the priest, came back with him and they both looked up at the ceiling. 'It's only damp, Mrs Rooney . . .' he said.

I had no serious illnesses as a kid, just the usual measles and chicken pox. But I remember one accident when I ripped open my knee on a fence – only I didn't tell my mum because I wasn't supposed to have climbed it. I still have the scar to this day.

When I was about six, the school doctor said I should wear glasses as I had a lazy eye. I got fitted up, and was given the specs which I had for about a year, but I always refused to wear them. Graeme also had to have glasses, but he was more willing than me and wore his for a few years.

I probably still have a slightly lazy left eye. I have got specs for reading but I hardly ever use them. I considered contact lenses, but I've been told they won't help because of the problem I have.

I did have a couple of playground fights while I was at St Swithin's. One was with a boy called Garry who was bigger than me, aged ten when I was nine. The fight ended even. The other was with a lad called Craig who was seen as cock of the school. His nickname was 'Psycho', similar to Stuart Pearce, the former England defender, but I caught him off-guard and landed a good blow. I think it began with an argument about football: was it a goal, or not? We both wanted to win so much.

On each of these occasions, the teachers came out into the playground, broke up the fight, and then sent for our mothers. I told my mum I was just doing what my dad had said, that I should stand up for myself, to hit

Our Lady & St. Swithin's R.C. Primary School

Report on ___Wayne Rooney___ Year __5__   Date 8th July 1996

Attendance: Possible- __358__   Actual- __324__   Unauthorised absences- ____   Late- __2__

	Achievements, Progress, Other Skills and Abilities
ENGLISH R.A. _3.6/3.9_ 1. Reading. 2. Writing. 3. Speaking and Listening.	Wayne's reading is showing real signs of improving. His understanding of the written word is deeper and this will, in time, help his written work. At the moment he has some good ideas, but sometimes finds it rather difficult to write them down. He has been rather reluctant to learn his spellings, which detracts from his creative writing, and he is sometimes careless when copying from a book or the board. Wayne is orally very confident and has made very good contributions to oral work. He must try to be more reliable about bringing his reading book and homework to school. Wayne's handwriting has improved considerably.
MATHEMATICS 1. Use of Number, Algebra and Measures. 2. Use of Shape, Space and Data Handling.	Wayne is quick and confident in Mathematics, but he sometimes tends to rush his work and this leads to careless mistakes. He grasps new concepts quite quickly and, if he can be persuaded to "slow down" and check his work, his progress will be even better in Year 6. Wayne has made excellent progress with learning his tables and this fluency has increased his ability with Mental Arithmetic. Sadly, Wayne's classroom achievements have not always been reflected in the homework he has produced.
SCIENCE 1. Scientific skills, exploration and investigation. 2. Knowledge and understanding of Science.	Wayne's deductive ability is developing well and he is interested in most areas of Science work. He makes some very interesting and thoughtful oral contributions, but must always guard against being distracted by what is going on around him. He sometimes loses concentration and as a result does not always work to the best of his ability and can exhibit silly behaviour. Wayne enjoys working in a group situation where he can be supported in the understanding of new concepts.

My Year 5 St Swithin's School report.

25

	Achievements, Progress, Other Skills and Abilities
RELIGIOUS EDUCATION	Very Good. Wayne shows a lively interest and takes an active part in all classroom discussions based on this subject.
TECHNOLOGY 1. Designing. 2. Use of Computers.	Wayne tries hard to produce a worthwhile end product. He prefers to work in a group where he can be encouraged and given support by other children. Wayne has good ideas but still needs time for his manual skills to develop. Wayne enjoys Information Technology and feels confident with computer work.
HISTORY	Wayne has a reasonable concept of times in the past and he is able to describe and discuss incidents in the Tudor period. His topic work was done to the best of his ability.
GEOGRAPHY	Wayne is making progress and does try to complete the set tasks. However, a lack of concentration sometimes means that work is incomplete. Orally, Wayne does very well, but presentation of written work can let him down.
ART	Unfortunately Wayne often rushes his work and does not always achieve the results he is aiming for. Wayne's lack of patience means he is often unable to produce the desired results.
MUSIC	Wayne is enthusiastic about all musical activities and performs well as part of a group. He finds listening to music more difficult than taking part.
PHYSICAL EDUCATION	Very Good. Wayne can be a little boisterous at times, and should learn to control this for safety reasons. However, his enthusiasm, energy and skill are a credit to him and he has a very good technique when using apparatus.
GENERAL PROGRESS -including Behaviour and Relationships.	Wayne is a very sociable boy who really enjoys the company of his classmates. His attitude to work can vary very much. He often does not listen to instructions he is given because he is "otherwise engaged." Most homework is done to a satisfactory standard, but not always brought to school on the right day. Wayne is a very friendly, outgoing person who always shows a great enjoyment of all physical activities.
OTHER ACHIEVEMENTS	Wayne has been a very valuable member of the Cross-Country and Athletics teams.
Teacher *Anne M. Robinson*	Headteacher *J. A. McCart*

My Year 5 St Swithin's School report (cont'd).

back if anyone ever struck me. That was my excuse for fighting. I was actually quite small and weedy at primary school, not one of the bigger boys. But I could stand up for myself.

For many years I had awful freckles. I hated them, wished they'd go away. My mother says she once caught me trying to get rid of them by scrubbing my face with a wire brush. I can't remember that, but it sounds likely. I was embarrassed because I felt they made me look so young and girlish. Eventually, though, they started to fade away.

On my last day at St Swithin's, when I was 11, all the girls were in tears as they bid the boys goodbye. We made sure we wouldn't be forgotten, though, by signing our names on each other's shirts.

I loved my time at St Swithin's and was sad to leave. I was also always happy at home. I suppose I was brought up in a tough area, with lots of poor families, but I wasn't aware of my family being poor. I seemed to get things like sweets or a bike or a football – if I cried long enough.

In the past, the estate had been very rough, and it became worse after I left, so I gather, but I wasn't aware of it being a bad place. I can only remember one occasion when the police came and blocked off our road. They were after an armed robber from our estate whom they'd been chasing, and managed to corner him in the youth club behind our house.

All told, my childhood was pretty ordinary, really. Nothing awful happened; just normal stuff, for the times, and for the sort of estate I lived on.

It seemed to me a very happy childhood, with loving, caring parents and lots of relatives I liked. Obviously there were family rows; various aunts would sometimes start shouting and swearing at each other, pulling each other's hair out, but next day they'd be the best of friends. That's what big families are like. Especially Irish families – if, of course, we are Irish. They might row amongst themselves, but they still stick together.

When I was young, as I said earlier, I needed a light on, or some sort of background noise, to help me sleep. Even now, when I'm on my own, I still not only like to have the TV and light on – but also a vacuum cleaner. Failing that, a fan or a hair dryer will do. I've ruined so many hair dryers by letting them burn out.

Coleen, my fiancée, hates it. She won't let me turn on a vacuum cleaner or a fan, not when we're together. But if she's away, or I'm away in a hotel with the team and in a bedroom of my own, to help me sleep I'll often switch on a fan or a hair dryer or the air-conditioning – any sort of machine which makes that sort of noise. So far I haven't set fire to anywhere.

I know it's stupid. But I don't really know the explanation. I've only ever met one person with the same habit, and that was a man who, when he was little, was carried in a sling by his mother. Often she would dry her hair while holding him, so he associated that noise with the comfort of his mother, and it helped him sleep.

I suppose many of us had silly, childhood habits which have taken us a long time to grow out of. At the age of 20, though, there's still time for me to grow out of mine . . .

TWO

Early Ball Skills

I was born a Blue. It was hard to avoid it, really, my family on both sides being die-hard Everton fans. But my dad wasn't simply a fan, following from afar – he went to every home match he possibly could.

I attended my first Everton match when I was only six months old and still in nappies. I don't know how my dad managed it as he didn't use a push-chair or a baby sling, which I think he would have refused to be seen with anyway. He had to carry me all the way, which involved two buses to get to the ground, and then hold me during the match while standing at the Gladys Street End. I was well-behaved, apparently, so from then on dad took me regularly. Even when I got a bit older, and was toddling about, I never moaned, cried or got bored during the game. I only played up, he says, on the way home after the game was over.

It was also at the age of six months that I first showed my ball skills, at least that's what my parents tell me.

When a ball was put into my arms I was able to hold on to it. At the same age, I could pick out colours. I'd be sat in my relaxer chair in front of the TV watching snooker and my eyes would light up when the players hit the different balls. Blue, of course, was the colour to which I reacted most.

At two, I was playing soccer and could volley the ball, so dad says, right to the end of the street where we lived. It couldn't have been a very long street.

I also used to volley the ball over my nan's fence, which was about six feet high, but would then have to scramble over it to get it back. Usually I couldn't climb back, though, and would just stand on the other side crying.

In all the photos of when I am little, I seem to be wearing an Everton strip of some sort. What a surprise. There's a snap of me, aged six months, looking very fat-faced and chubby with a large blue rosette which reads, 'Everton to win TODAY'. This was a free rosette, given out with *The Today* newspaper on the day of the 1986 FA Cup final at Wembley against Liverpool. Everton were beaten 3–1, a result we still don't talk about in our house.

On my first birthday, I wore the full Everton kit. For my present my dad gave me an Everton sign, in the style of a yellow car number plate. Someone in his local pub made them so he bought one, for himself really, but he gave it to me anyway. I kept it in my bedroom throughout my childhood, and took it with me when we moved to Stonebridge Lane in 1998, a bigger council house with four bedrooms and a parlour. Today, the sign takes pride of place in the glass front door at my dad's house. He kept hold of it when I moved out, which shows he always had his eye on it.

I always had a party for my birthday, as did my two brothers. Mum did us proud, providing a sit-down tea, table cloth, place names, ice cream and jelly, jaffa cakes, and games. There were always lots of kids invited, most of them our cousins.

My bedroom was decorated with Everton memorabilia, from the bedside lamp shade to the wallpaper. Posters showed off all my heroes, particularly my favourite player, Duncan Ferguson. He was a hard man and I liked the way he always gave his best.

I can't remember much about those early Everton games I attended with my dad, but as I got older, I used to hang around the stadium after the matches and try to get autographs.

When Duncan went to prison, after he was involved in a fight, I wrote to him twice. I think I must have been aged about nine. I told him he shouldn't be in jail, and that me and my mates were desperate for him to come back and play for Everton. He actually wrote back, thanking me for my letter, and I was made up. He had no idea who I was, of course, and I presumed he replied to all the fans who wrote to him.

Early Ball Skills

At primary school, after my first two weeks when I talked only to the girls, I played football in the playground all the time. At home, too, I used to get up early and be out in the street from seven o'clock, playing with my cousins before going to school. After school, I'd nip over our garden fence and play on the five-a-side pitch at the Gems. I'd often play on my own, shooting in, even when it got dark. They had floodlights, but not, of course, for a kid shooting in on his own.

It's interesting that the older players nowadays often bemoan the fact that street football has died out, due to the amount of traffic and the worries about child security, but I endlessly played in the street with my mates without a problem. And only five years ago at that.

My Uncle Eugene, who often spoiled me, bought me my first leather ball. From then on he had to buy me another one every week, as I wore them out so quickly by playing in the street or on the tarmac five-a-side pitch. And it was Uncle Eugene who took me abroad for the first time, to Disneyland Paris, with his family when I was about eight.

The first proper team I played for was a kids' side, run by the Western pub where my dad used to drink, and which played in an Under-12s league. Most of the pubs on our estate had boys' teams. I first turned out for them when I was seven and scored the winning goal. I also played for several other teams, such as Pye. But I only once played for my primary school team,

St Swithin's, because during my time there they didn't have a proper team.

Copplehouse, another pub team, was my main club which I joined when I was eight and which played in an Under-9s league.

As a kid, I admit I never thought about becoming a professional footballer, even for Everton. I dreamed about scoring goals, and about the Blues winning games, like most other kids – although I'm sure they don't all dream about Everton. It honestly never entered my head that I could possibly be a real player.

However, one day, when I was aged nine playing for Copplehouse, it turned out that scouts from both Liverpool and Everton were watching the game. After the match, the Liverpool scout approached my dad and asked me if I'd like to have a trial.

So two days later, after school, I went along to Melwood, Liverpool's training ground. I don't recall who took me – but I know I was wearing my Everton kit.

Unfortunately, I didn't hit it off with the Liverpool coaches who were a bit funny towards me. I don't know why, but perhaps it had something to do with wearing the Everton colours. I didn't wear the shirt as a defiant gesture, I just always wore it. After school, I lived in my Everton shirt.

There were about 30 kids at the hour-long trial, all aged around nine. We practised our skills and technique, then we had some five-a-side games. I must have impressed some of them because, afterwards, I was asked to attend another trial the following week. Naturally, I said yes.

In the meantime, my dad received a phone call from Bob Pendleton, the Everton scout who had seen me play for Copplehouse. Everton also wanted me to attend a trial – but it was scheduled for the same evening as my second Liverpool trial. Despite that, I went to Bellefield, Everton's training ground, rather than Liverpool's. That was that. Once Everton had appeared interested there was no choice to be had.

Dad came with me on the bus, secretly hoping to meet Joe Royle, the then Everton manager. It was a similar sort of trial, with about 30 kids taking part in skills exercises, but this time I loved everything about it: the people, the coaches and the atmosphere. There were, of course, loads of other kids, like me, who had turned up in their Everton shirts.

To be fair, Liverpool had probably been just as good to me and I felt my trial with them had gone well. But, being all emotional about Everton, I decided they were so much better and I felt more at home with them.

Straight after that first Everton trial, the club spoke to my dad, and asked him there and then if I would sign schoolboy forms. Of course, we said yes.

Had Liverpool asked me to sign first and not have another trial, then I'm sure I would have signed for them and been a 'Red'. I think their system was to ask you along to several trials before deciding whether or not to make an offer. Or perhaps they simply weren't sure about me. Anyway, that was that. Aged nine, I was about to join Everton.

I rushed home from Bellefield to tell my mum. She wasn't in as she'd gone to church, the Queen of Martyrs, to take part in a rehearsal for Graeme's communion. She happened to be sitting next to Franny Jeffers's mother as I ran in, and when I told her my news she burst into tears.

Franny, like me, attended De La Salle secondary school, lived locally, and went on to play for Everton – as had, earlier on, Mick Lyons and Paul Jewell, now manager of Wigan. But, being four years older than me, I never actually came across Franny at school as he left just as I arrived.

I went and told all my mates who were well chuffed for me. To celebrate, we had a kick-around in the street as usual.

I received the official letter from Everton a few days later, in April 1995, and which my mum still has. The club offered me a place for the 1995/96 season at their Centre of Excellence as it was called in those days; later, while I was still there, it became the Everton Football Academy.

The letter said how pleased they were with me, that I would form part of 'our special group of Centre of Excellence players' and that I had to 'set and main-

RH/JMF

GOODISON PARK
LIVERPOOL L4 4EL
Tel. (Administration)
0151 521 2020
Fax 0151 523 9666
Tel. (Box Office)
0151 523 6666
Fax 0151 524 0550

April 1995

Wayne Rooney
28 Armill Road
Croxteth
Liverpool
L11 4TR

Dear Wayne,

Everton Football Club: Centre of Excellence

On behalf of Everton Football Club I am very pleased
to be able to offer you a place at our Centre of
Excellence for Season 1995/6.

The coaching staff have been very happy with your
progress since joining us. As a consequence you will
now form an important part of our special group of
Centre of Excellence players and to this end you will
need to set and maintain excellent examples to your
fellow pupils at school and clubs. If you or your
parents would at any time like to discuss your
progress please contact me whenever it is convenient
on 0151 228 3174.

May I request your assistance in completing the
attached form and forward it by return of post in the
enclosed stamped addressed envelope.

Yours sincerely,

RAY HALL
Youth Development Officer

Secretary
M.J. DUNFORD
Manager
J. ROYLE

Registered Number
36624, England

The letter from Everton offering me a place at their Academy.

tain excellent examples to fellow pupils at school and clubs.'

All that summer I remember being so excited, hardly able to wait for the new season to begin. I suppose it was only then, knowing I had joined Everton as a school boy, that I began to think I might actually become a professional footballer. Grown-ups started telling me that if I worked hard and practised I could make it. Someone has to, so why not me? I suppose hundreds, if not thousands, of kids think that every year.

I started with Everton, at nine, with 15 other boys of my age and we were classed as the Under-10s. As with all Academies, which most professional clubs now have, players of the same year stick together for training sessions and don't mix with the other years, far less the professional players. Hopefully, you then progress through the years. It's like school in that sense, with tests and assessments at the end of each year; except that, unlike school, you get kicked out for good if you don't do well enough.

I attended training three times a week after school, on Monday, Wednesday and Friday, from 5 to 6.30pm. Sunday mornings saw us play against an Academy side of our age group from another club in the North West. If we were playing away, we got picked up by a coach at Bellefield.

Each session, my dad or mum took me to Bellefield. In the early years, when we didn't have a car, we went on the bus or walked as it wasn't too far away. They would then wait to bring me back. Parents have to be as keen as their kids, making sure they turn up on time, and with the right kit. Some, of course, are even keener than their kids, shouting and screaming on the touchline. I owe a lot to my parents, as well as to Everton, for all their years of support, trailing back and forth with me.

After football training, I also went boxing. At roughly the same time as I started with Everton I joined a boys' boxing club, run by my Uncle Ritchie, dad's brother, at Croxteth Sports Centre. We just did sparring and training. I enjoyed it and although I never actually fought in any matches, I was good at attacking people and had a strong punch.

I loved the football training. We learned a lot of technical skills, like kicking the ball with the outside of the foot. I'm naturally right-footed, and the coaches worked on my left, so I would be able to use that just as well.

I was about average size and weight, but some of the kids in the Everton Under-10s were much bigger than me. There were also one or two whom I thought were better than me, such as Joseph Jones, a calm midfielder and a very good passer of the ball.

However, seeing one or two kids who were better made me try even harder. I wanted to show off what skills I had and so became very ball-greedy. I went for goal whenever I could and wouldn't pass. The coaches would shout at me, 'Lay it off!' while my dad shouted 'Take him on!' Instead, I would do neither: I'd let rip a shot from the edge of the area and try to score from 30 yards. Which I often did. It was all part of trying to impress, to show them how good I was.

At the end of that first year at Everton, each of us received a written assessment; I was adjudged 'Very Good' for control, passing, stamina, strength, speed and positional sense.

Under the heading of Attitude the report said, 'Does listen, but he dreams about goals, and everything is geared to the back of the net. Great will to win and Wayne has made efforts to work on his build-up play.'

Under Progress and Overall Observations, it remarked, 'Works hard and listens to the coaches. Build-up play is coming on and his left side is developing well. Great motivation and the best natural goalscorer I've seen. Technically, he does things ahead of his years and has good fast feet. Hope he develops physically and does not get overplayed.'

The assessment was stamped by Ray Hall, the Youth Development officer, but hand-written by Andy Windsor, one of the coaches.

During that first season playing for Everton's Centre of Excellence Under-10 team and sometimes the Under-11s, dad kept a detailed record of all the games I took part in. I wasn't really aware at the time that he

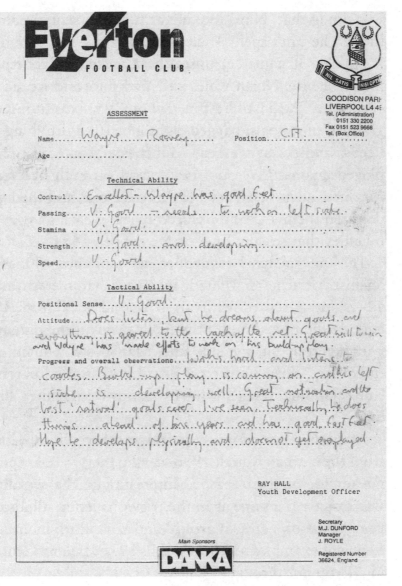

The assessment from the Everton Academy.

was doing that. Now, looking at it, it's amazingly neat, though he can't spell 'Anglesy' [sic].

I played 30 games, against other Centres of Excellence in Lancashire, North Wales and Yorkshire and scored in each one. Against Preston, whom we beat 15–0, I grabbed nine goals, bagged eight in a 10–5 drubbing of Leeds, and six as we beat Manchester United 12–2. I played against Liverpool twice, and on each occasion for our Under-11s. They beat us once 6–2 and then we defeated them 4–3 and I scored twice in each game. All together that season, I netted a total of 114 goals.

The only match I remember now, of those 30, was against Manchester United, when we hammered them 12–2 and I scored with an overhead kick from the edge of the box. Around the pitch were all the parents, with Everton on one side and Manchester United on the other. When I scored, I heard both sets of parents start clapping. That's why I'll always remember that day.

After that first year I received another official letter from the club, in March 1996, saying they were keeping me on for another season. Interestingly, the wording was exactly the same as in the previous letter, all about being 'part of a special group' and having to 'maintain excellent examples to fellow pupils'. The standard wording if you got through, I guess.

When I began that second season, I was thrilled to find I'd been promoted. Instead of being with the

	EVERTON U10 - SEASON 1995-96							
1	EVERTON	4	ST HELENS	1	WAYNE	115	3	
2	EVERTON	4	BURY	0	WAYNE		4	
3	EVERTON	7	CHESTER	1	WAYNE		6	
4	EVERTON	4	BLACKPOOL	2	WAYNE		2	
5	EVERTON	15	PRESTON	0	WAYNE		9	
6	EVERTON	5	ELSMERE PORT	2	WAYNE		2	
7	EVERTON	5	LEEDS	2	WAYNE		3	
8	EVERTON	8	N. FOREST.	0	WAYNE		3	
9	EVERTON	6	BURY	2	WAYNE		2	
10	EVERTON	12	MAN, UNITED	2	WAYNE		6	
11	EVERTON	2	LIVERPOOL	6	WAYNE	11	2	
12	EVERTON	4	LIVERPOOL	3	WAYNE	11	2	
13	EVERTON	7	N FOREST	2	WAYNE		5	
14	EVERTON	2	N FOREST	1	WAYNE		2	
15	EVERTON	0	BURY	0	WAYNE		0	
16	EVERTON	10	PRESTON	1	WAYNE		5	
17	EVERTON	8	CROSBY BOYS	2	WAYNE		6	
18	EVERTON	9	PRESTON	1	WAYNE		6	
19	EVERTON	10	LEEDS	5	WAYNE		8	
20	EVERTON	6	N, COUNTY	4	WAYNE		3	
21	EVERTON	8	BLACKPOOL	1	WAYNE		3	
22	EVERTON	10	PRESTON	2	WAYNE		6	
23	EVERTON	13	N, FOREST	1	WAYNE		3	
24	EVERTON	3	N, FOREST	0	WAYNE		1	
25	EVERTON	5	TRANMERE	0	WAYNE		2	
26	EVERTON	9	BURY	1	WAYNE		6	
27	EVERTON	7	PETEBORO	0	WAYNE		3	
28	EVERTON	13	ANGLESEA	0	WAYNE		8	
29	EVERTON	9	ANGLESEA	0	WAYNE		4	TOTAL
30	EVERTON				WAYNE			114

Dad's handwritten record of my goals for Everton boys 1995/96.

Under-11s, as I'd expected, I had jumped two years and was put with the Under-12s. At the time, when that new season began in August 1996, I was still only 10 years old.

Every season, in each year group, there are five or six kids who get released. It's done quietly, one to one, with the youngster and his parents being taken aside from the rest of the group. It's only later that you realise that certain kids have gone when they are no longer turning up. Joseph Jones, for one, did make it through with me each year, until the very end.

The Everton Academy, like most others, has nine years, right up to Under-19, which usually means a total of 140 boys attend the Academy at any one time guided by 24 full-time staff. I'm told it works out at a cost of £10,000 a year for each boy – most of whom never make it.

Up to the age of 16, the Academy boys are not paid, of course, although their parents may get travelling expenses for long-distance games plus a few first-team tickets every season.

It's not just a matter of basic talent, or even keenness and dedication, that decides who will come through. Boys grow and develop at different times, in different ways.

The big problem comes when a youngster reaches 13 or 14. Other distractions come along: they want to go out with their mates or chase girls. They want to do loads of other things with their spare time, play with computers or whatever, rather than trail across town in the dark on a cold winter's evening to train.

With me, though, once I got started I only ever lived for football.

THREE

A *Jingle in Secondary School*

The secondary school I went to was called De La Salle, a Roman Catholic comprehensive with about 1,000 kids, all boys. I didn't have much interest in academic subjects as, by then, I was determined to succeed in football. But I was always well behaved and didn't cause trouble or muck around in class. I just didn't bother that much with things like homework, although my reports were never really bad.

My Year 8 report, from July 1999 when I was 13, said I was late 51 times and my attendance was pretty poor, managing only 286 half-days out of a possible 320. The form tutor's comments mention that I have to 'improve my punctuality'. I don't think I ever did.

The Geography exam consisted of three tests and apparently I got a total of nothing. I didn't turn up for any of them, so that could explain it. At least I was consistent.

I also got 0 per cent in Spanish. If only I had done

DE LA SALLE SCHOOL
SCHOOL REPORT
SUMMER TERM 1999

PUPIL'S NAME... WAYNE ROONEY...

FORM...... 8B.

Signed... K Nolan

Headteacher/Deputy Headteacher

My De La Salle School report.

German, I might have been really fluent and able to amaze them all in Germany...

Other marks were 36 per cent in Art, 39 per cent in English, 40 per cent in Maths, 49 per cent in Science and 54 per cent in History. Not bad. My best result, though, was in RE in which I scored 63 per cent. 'There are times,' the RE report says, 'when Wayne is a model pupil.' So there you are, then. It shows I could do it, when I could be bothered.

However, there was one awful remark in that report which, in hindsight, now looks much more serious than it did to me at the time.

In the overall comments for the year it said that I must 'get to class without any distractions, i.e. gambling.' It makes me sound like a real gambling addict, wasting

General Progress Report	Year Ending:- July 1999

Name: WAYNE ROONEY   **Year:** 8   **Form:** 8

Attendance (half days): **Actual** 286   **Possible** 320   = 89.38 %

No of Unauthorised Absences: 0   **No of Lates:** 51

General Progress and Achievements (including Public Examinations if applicable)
  SEE SUBJECT REPORTS.

Targets for Attendance and Punctuality:
  INCREASE ATTENDANCE TO 91%.

General Targets:
  GET TO CLASS WITHOUT ANY DISTRACTIONS, ie GAMBLING.
                Signed (Form Tutor) MWB

An excellent representative for the school. He must improve his punctuality.
                Signed (Head of Year)

My General Progress report.

all my time and money – as if I had any to spend at the age of 13.

All I was doing was playing a game called 'Jingle' in the playground. You stood in a line with your mates and each would throw a 10 or a 50p piece, or whatever we'd have, against the wall. You had to land your coin as near to the wall as possible and the person whose coin ended nearest won all the money. Sometimes I won, sometimes I didn't, it wasn't a huge amount either way; perhaps £1 at the most, which my mother had given me for the school tuck shop.

There was a craze amongst my mates for a while to play Jingle every breaktime – only the teachers used

Subject: Physical Education	Key Stage 3	Year Ending:- July 1999

Name: WAYNE ROONEY   Form: 8 B   Group: Mr WILLIAMS

Course Content:
At the end of Year 8 your son will have completed the second year of his KS3 National Curriculum PE studies. He has been assessed, by his teachers, in his ability to:
  i)   Devise and adapt strategies and tactics across appropriate activities.
  ii)   Adapt and refine existing skills and develop new skills safely across the activities.
  iii)   Understand and evaluate how well they and others have achieved in what they set out to do.
Your son has achieved the following level

C	Working beyond the level expected for KS3		
B	Working at the level expected for KS3		✓
A	Working towards the level expected for KS3		

Targets: WAYNE IS A VERY ABLE SPORTSMAN WHO'S WORKED HARD THROUGHOUT THE YEAR. HE NEEDS TO MAINTAIN THIS LEVEL OF WORK NEXT YEAR   Signature *P. Williams*

My PE report.

to hate us doing it; they'd rush out and try to break it up. Eventually, we got bored and turned to other playground games.

Very often I'd use it as an excuse for being late into class, saying I had been carried away playing Jingle and forgot the time, which wasn't always true. It was part of not being really bothered with lessons.

When I was at primary school I received free school dinners because my dad was jobless for long periods and my mother, having three young kids to look after, couldn't work. But when I started at De La Salle, my mother took a job as a school dinner lady there. I liked that as I got good portions – but we had to pay for the

Subject: MFL Spanish			Year Ending:- July 1999		
Name: WAYNE ROONEY		Form: 8B		Teacher: MISS G. GREAVES	
Course Content: Topic areas this year have been School, Food and Drink, Hobbies (Sport / Music / Clothes). (Some groups have also studied House and Home) The Liverpool Scheme of Work is followed in Key Stage 3, which draws on various coursebook sources. Whenever possible tape and video supplement the course.					
	Excellent	Very Good	Good	Satisfactory	Poor
Completion of Classwork:					✓
Standard of Classwork:					✓
Standard of Homework:					✓
Attitude					✓
Targets: Wayne should not allow silly behaviour to distract him from producing his best work. He should try to concentrate more fully in class					
Exam Result 0 %		**Working at NC Level** 1		Signed *G. Greaves*	

My Spanish report. Don't look.

dinners as we now had an income. In fact, we had two as my mother also got a cleaning job, working at the school after it had finished for the day.

She had these two jobs all through my childhood. They didn't pay much – I think as a dinner lady she got £100 a week – but it was enough to provide me with pocket money, and I always had a bike of some sort, such as a BMX, on which I did wheelies round the estate, or a mountain bike. For a time I also had a little motorbike, something called a Yamaha PW80, which had three gears and no clutch. I didn't have a licence for it or sit any test – I just rode it round the estate when there were no policemen around.

50

It was great that both my younger brothers, Graeme and John, were also taken on in turn by the Everton Academy. When the Academy system – a national network under the FA – was introduced, one of the rules was that kids had to live no more than an hour's car ride from the club's training ground. This was to prevent them having to travel huge distances. In big places with lots of clubs, like London, Merseyside or Tyneside, the competition was very intense, and identifying possible talent at a young age was common. Graeme and John were thrilled, of course, as was I and the whole Everton-mad Rooney clan.

But it meant my dad had to spend even more time running us around. It became, in effect, his job as he could hardly fit in normal work on a building site, not that he was being offered much anyway.

One day, at Bellefield, the three of us, all in our Everton kits, had our photograph taken with my hero, Duncan Ferguson. On the picture he's bending down with his arms round me and Graeme, and we're all so titchy compared to him. I don't think he knew who I was or had even talked to me before. The reason for the photograph was that we were three brothers, all signed as Everton schoolboys at the same time, which was unusual.

Graeme and John seemed to do well, but I suppose it was hard for them with me ahead doing particularly well, especially when I was put up by two years.

When John was about nine, Everton told him he was putting on weight and had to go on a diet with special training. My mum was really furious. When John told her he had to train in the gym on his own, without any of the other kids, she went up to the club to protest that it was victimisation. But the club said no, they were simply helping him with individual treatment.

Luckily, I never suffered weight problems. I was so dedicated, so keen to do well and impress everybody, and I did what I was told because I loved every moment of playing football.

I never cut myself off from mates on the estate, though, and they were still my best friends. When I was about 13 I went with a group which had somehow got hold of a bottle of cider, and we stood behind the pub drinking it – but it didn't do anything for me and I refused any more.

Some people on the estate moved on to smoking weed and sniffing glue, but I never did any of that. I tried to smoke an ordinary cigarette once, but never liked it. I've never taken drugs of any sort, although, like everyone else, I knew who the dealers and druggies were on our estate.

Sadly, some of the kids I knocked around with on the estate became addicts. There's one or two I see now, when I go back – they're still on drugs and look terrible.

It was partly wanting to be fit for football, that was

one reason I never got involved, and also because I was scared my mum would find out. She would have battered me, although more likely my dad and uncles. Yes, my family would definitely have given me a slap if they'd heard I'd been taking drugs.

Until I was about 15 I never even swore at home as I knew mum would tell me off. However, I did most of the other things that the ordinary kids did on our estate, such as hanging around the chip shop and the street corners, eyeing up the girls. I had my first so-called girlfriend when I was about 13. I went out with her for about two months. I also had another girlfriend for a while with whom I went out for about seven months. I must have been 15 by then.

The girl I always really really fancied, though, from about 13 was Coleen McLoughlin. She was at our sister school, St John Bosco High, a girls' comprehensive. At De La Salle, I often used to have arguments with the other lads about her when we'd sit and discuss who were the best-looking girls at St John Bosco. I always thought Coleen was the most fit and would stick up for her.

I knew her brothers, and she knew my cousins, but I never seemed to get the chance to speak to her properly, far less ask her out. I was too shy, I suppose, and too scared. I also knew she was a keen student who did her homework properly – unlike me.

*   *   *

One of the perks of being at Everton's Academy, apart from the fact that you and your parents each received the odd free ticket for matches at Goodison, was the chance to be a ball boy. I did that for two seasons, when I was 10 and 11. Ball boys had to be members of the Everton World Wide Fan Club, which I was, but the club usually made sure that the Academy kids had the first chances.

I well remember my ball boy debut. We were getting beaten 1–0, then towards the end of the game we equalised. Soon afterwards, the ball went out of play for a goal kick, on my side of the pitch, not far from Neville Southall in goal. I took my time getting the ball, thinking we were now playing for a draw. Suddenly, I heard Neville screaming at me, 'F***ing hurry up, ball boy!' I was shitting myself as I raced to return it as quickly as I could.

When I served as ball boy, we were always supposed to throw it back into play, not kick it, but I never did. When a ball rolls along the ground to me my natural reaction is to kick it, not pick it up. I always kicked it – and always got told off afterwards. But my kicking was so good that it was quicker and more direct than throwing it; if it was a throw-in I could kick it straight into the player's hands.

I acted as a mascot once, when I was 10. It was a derby game against Liverpool, so I was dead excited. I got to the stadium really early – only to find it had been called off because heavy rain meant the pitch was waterlogged. I was so disappointed.

The game was rescheduled for a month or so later. Before kick-off me and the Liverpool mascot were pictured as always in the centre-circle with the captains and officials. Dave Watson was the Everton captain that day and John Barnes the skipper of Liverpool. Looking at the photo now, I can't believe how thin and weedy I was, as well as a bit scruffy, with my socks round my ankles. The Liverpool mascot had blonde hair and looked like a girl, but, in fact, was a boy.

As a mascot, you are allowed to shoot in before the game begins. The goalkeeper lobs the ball to you, about six yards away, so you can't miss it. Usually, the mascot grits his teeth and tries to side foot it straight at the goal, but it often just trickles and doesn't even reach the keeper. Or he runs at it full-pelt but often misses it completely as he's so nervous.

What I did was to chip Neville Southall from outside the penalty area. Once the ball went straight over his head and another time it clipped the crossbar. I'd been practising all week, knowing what I was going to do, just to be different. But Neville wasn't at all amused and, I think, called me a flash bastard.

About a year ago, an interesting thing happened. That game against Liverpool in 1996 was, at the time, shown live on Sky TV although they didn't, of course, show

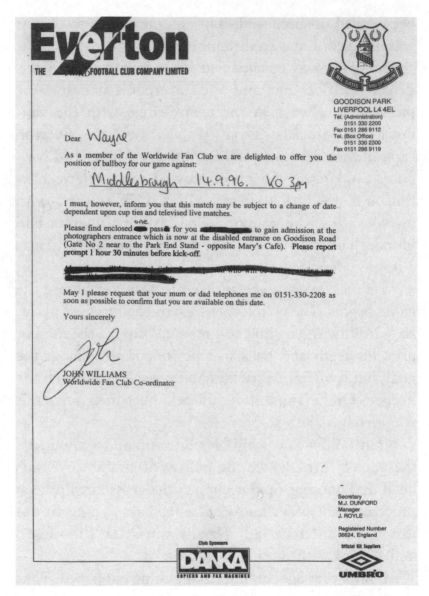

My invitation to become a ballboy at Goodison Park.

the mascots kicking in beforehand. Nine years on, for some reason, Sky decided to wind back the tape from that day – and someone recognised me. I've seen the tape – and I can clearly be seen chipping Neville. No wonder Neville wasn't amused . . .

FOUR

Always a Blue?

I was doing well at Everton's Centre of Excellence, just loving it, and getting excellent assessments each year. I'd had no problems being put up a year with lads two years older. When I reached 14, the club increased the training from three nights a week to four, but I didn't mind that either – I always loved training.

We had to attend on a Monday as well as Tuesday, Wednesday and Thursday. For the Monday session, a room was put aside after training and we were all supposed to sit and do our school homework having brought it with us. I always used to say I had none.

I never had trouble with the other lads, even when put in with an older group. I suppose it could have been awkward, playing for the Under-15s when I was only 12, or the Under-17s when I was 15, and they might have muttered to themselves, 'Who's this kid, who's he think he is?' Perhaps there was a bit of jealousy, I don't know, but once they saw me play I was okay. And I usually became the best in the group by the end of each season, or so I liked to think.

However, around the age of 13 or 14, two things began to go wrong. A new coach started taking us for training and I didn't like him. He seemed too pushy and bossy, telling me what to do all the time, and appeared to have it in for me. I didn't react well. Until then the coaches had always been nice and every one seemed to like me, and I liked them. This was the first unlikeable one I'd come across. I gave him a bit of lip, which, of course, I shouldn't have done, so that didn't help.

One day he told me I had to train with the defenders and practise defending. I gave him a mouthful and told him I wasn't doing that: 'I'm a striker, I want to practise striking.' In that case, he replied, I would not be in the team for Sunday's game.

I came home, moaned to my mum and told her I was going to pack it in if he continued. I wasn't enjoying it any more.

This problem went on for quite a while – in fact I was unhappy for most of the season because of him. I didn't like him, I was convinced he didn't like me, and I thought his training methods were boring.

In the end, my dad could see what was happening, as he usually watched the training. He knew how I felt, but he also realised what this coach was trying to achieve. He gave me a talking to, said the coach knew what he was doing and I had to do what he said, not be cheeky. They'd been training schoolkids for years. It was all for my good. So, in the end, I did as he said and put up with it.

I'm sure, looking back, it probably was my fault. The coach's dislike of me was in my head – and I made it worse by being bolshy. Now, of course, I'm grateful for defending practice and I like to think, for a striker, I'm a good defender.

The other thing that went wrong was to do with my knees. I had started to wake up with this hellish pain in both, I could hardly get out of bed, and it was agony walking to school. Sometimes my knees were so full of fluid they had to be drained. It took about an hour and half each day for the pain to start fading.

It got worse and my knees became painful in the evenings when I was training with Everton. I didn't tell anyone for several months, as I was worried it would affect my football career, so I just played on through the pain.

I also began to get pains in my back. I think for a while it affected my game: my balance was possibly not as good as it had been and my progress was not as rapid as from the age of 9 to 14. In fact, that could have been why the coach was so hard on me, worried that I might begin to fade, something which happens to lots of lads aged about 14; they show brilliant promise at nine, are clearly much better than other kids of their age, then their progress slows down as they get older and the others catch up.

I eventually told the Everton physio about the problem – and he immediately exclaimed, 'Ossie Schlatter' [as in Osgood-Schlatter Disease]. I thought it was some German bloke, but it's actually to do with growing pains; when bones are soft and still growing they can get injured easily and inflamed. They said I shouldn't worry – knee pains were normal for lads of 14 or so, who had been quite small and weedy but have then suddenly started shooting up in size.

When I started to have the back pains as well, the club told me to give up the boxing. They said I couldn't do both. So I stopped going to the boxing club and just concentrated on football. And what the physios said actually came true; after that year, the pains faded away and I've never suffered knee or back pain since, touch wood.

During that difficult year, I seemed to develop a terrible temper and found myself getting into lots of fights on the pitch. If I made a mistake, I'd throw myself into a tackle and commit a foul, or if some bigger, older lad on the other team was trying to rough me up, I'd react and punch him one.

In those youth games you didn't receive a red card. The referee would just signal to the bench that you had 'lost it' and they would substitute you. I'd then storm off the pitch straight into the dressing room. But it was all down to this mad desire to win, that's all.

I also got involved in a few fights at De La Salle. My school reports were still okay, apart from my doing much work, and none said I had played up or was badly behaved.

However, one day I kicked a hole in the wall of the science lab. I couldn't play footie for De La Salle, apart from in the first year, as the Everton Academy would not allow it, although I obviously played all the time in the school playground. One day, I came into the science lesson, still bouncing my best football, and the teacher took it off me, confiscated it. That was when I went mad and kicked the wall in, making a big hole.

When it was discovered, my mum and dad were sent for. I was still claiming it wasn't me – until they examined my shoes. The wall was made of hardboard plaster which was why I'd been able to kick such a big hole in it; but my shoe still had plaster all over it. So I had to confess it had been me. I was suspended from school for two days after that.

I also got in a fight with an older boy, a lad in the sixth form, when I was about 13. I had pinched his school bag in the playground, just for a laugh, and ran off with it. He chased after me and turned out to be a good runner, so he caught up. We had a fight: I won and he got a black eye. No, the teachers never found out, and he didn't report me; he was too embarrassed, I suppose, about being beaten up by a younger kid.

In the end, instead of getting into fights, either at school or on the pitch, I learned to keep calm. By nature, I am very laid back, lazy really, and not bothered by most things and most people. On the pitch, I made a point of keeping away from the 'heavies' when I was off the ball, and instead looked for space, ready to get in behind them.

When I was 12 and a half, playing for Liverpool Schools against Wolverhampton Schools, I apparently attracted the interest of some scouts from Wolves. After the game, they approached my dad and asked if I'd be interested in joining them. But he made it clear I'd signed for Everton; I was on their books, at their Centre of Excellence, and wanted to stay there.

I didn't actually know anything about this at the time. But Everton were furious when they heard, and my dad had to sign a legal document confirming he'd been approached by these two officials.

As I progressed, and started playing for the Under-15s and then the Under-17s, I began attracting interest from other big clubs – but, again, no-one told me. Even if they had, I wouldn't have been interested.

I went on my first overseas tour with Everton in 1998 when I was still 13. We played in a tournament in Switzerland against youth teams from Brazil and France, as well as the host nation; I think the French team was either Lyons or Auxerre. I was made the Everton captain, and we won the cup.

We stayed at a school and they put us up in some sort of nuclear shelter. Everyone slept in the same dorm and

Youth Department

GOODISON PARK
LIVERPOOL L4 4EL
Tel. (Administration)
0151 330 2200

Statement from Mr. W. Rooney, 23 Armill Road, Liverpool, L11 4TR

The following is a statement supplied by Mr. Wayne Rooney concerning his son Wayne Rooney.

At a game played at Bilston between Wolverhampton Schools U11s and Liverpool Schools U11s I was approached by two representatives from Wolverhampton Wanderers, one of whom I believed to be Mr. C. Evans, Youth Development Officer.

At the half-time interval during the game Team Managers of Liverpool Schools U11s, Mr. T. O'Keefe and Mr. R. Johnson, were approached by the officials from Wolverhampton Wanderers and were asked whether Wayne Rooney and Jay Smith were registered at Football Clubs. The information that Wayne is at Everton Football Club and Jay is at Liverpool Football Club was related to them. At the end of the game I was approached by, I believe, Mr. Chris Evans and an associate. (I had previously been told by Mr. O'Keefe and Mr. Johnson that these two gentlemen had made enquiries about my son and were told that he was at Everton Football Club). Mr. Evans asked me if Wayne would like to take a look around Wolverhampton Wanderers and that he would pay his expenses (and look after him). I indicated that Wayne was happy at Everton Football Club to which he suggested that if the situation changes would I contact Wolverhampton Wanderers on the phone number that was left with me.

Signed....................................... Date: 23rd March 1998

"BELLEFIELD TRAINING GROUND"
SANDFORTH ROAD
WEST DERBY
LIVERPOOL L12 1LL
Tel: 0151-282 1580
Fax: 0151-282 1590

Secretary
M.J. DUNFORD
Manager
H. KENDALL

Registered Number
36624, England

Official Kit Supplier

Official Club Sponsor
one2one

UMBRO
Only Football

The statement from my Dad about the approach from Wolves.

Ray Hall, who was in charge of us, said I kept everyone awake at night by talking in my sleep. I was probably scoring goals.

The thing about going abroad, we were told, was that it would give us an experience of foreign food and foreign places. Personally I hated all the foreign food, especially the bread. Ugh! All that lumpy brown stuff.

We also flew to the USA to take part in a tournament in Dallas. We stayed there for about two weeks and each of us was homed by local families connected with the Dallas youth soccer teams.

Beforehand, we each had to send off an individual letter about ourselves so we could be placed with the most suitable family. Now, when I look at my letter again, I think it's pretty clear the club must have helped us all write them. We had to list things like hobbies, so I put in fishing which I don't think I'd ever done much. I also said I liked Oasis so that bit was true.

The family I stayed with in Dallas was very nice. They had a bigger, posher home than our Croxteth council house, and had a son of my age and a younger daughter. For the first two days I was so homesick I couldn't eat. I didn't like their sandwiches and hated the waffle things and other stuff they had for breakfast. But it got a bit better. They were very kind and took me to a rodeo with other boys and girls – some of the girls were dressed as cowgirls. I enjoyed all that.

* * *

To my foster parent`s,

My name is Wayne Rooney and I am 13 year`s old. I live with my Mum and Dad and my two brother`s, Graeme and John. Both me and my brother`s play for Everton F.C. I play for under 14`s, Graeme plays for under 11`s and John plays for under 8`s. I play centre forward. I enjoy swimming, basketball and fishing but these are all second to my main love which is football. I like listening to music especially Oasis. I attend De La Salle High School for boy`s which is quite near to my house.

I was delighted when I heard that our team was visiting Dallas, and I can`t wait to get there. This is just a short introduction to myself, I am really looking forward to meeting you. If you wish to seek any further information please contact the above.

Thanking You

Wayne Rooney

My letter to the foster family in Dallas.

I think the first time I realised I might be special as a footballer was when I was 15 and in my last year at school. It wasn't that I had done anything major, not at this particular time, but I suddenly heard that De La Salle would be letting me off school for three days a week so I could train full-time at Everton.

I recently talked to Ray Hall, who is still in charge of Everton's Academy, and he confirmed it was the club that approached the school asking if I could have, first, one day off a week and later up to three, for full-time training.

I was also pleased when Ray told me that over the six years I was in his Academy, he couldn't remember me giving him 'an ounce of trouble.' He has no memory of me falling out with that coach so it couldn't have been very serious.

But he remembers one incident when I was about 15, and already making a bit of a name for myself locally as a youth player. He received a call at the training ground from a busy-body member of the public saying I was sitting in a pub, the Dog and Gun. Ray didn't check himself, but sent a coach round to the pub to do so. I was there – but I wasn't drinking at all, just sitting watching the football on TV.

That 'special' treatment happened when I was in my last term at school, about to leave at Easter. So I wouldn't be missing much. I was now playing for the Under-19 team and I was due to take part in some important FA Youth Cup games, along with players who had already left school and signed professional forms.

Until then, I hadn't thought of myself as a special player. I knew I was good, always keen to win, and even keener to show off how good I was. But being allowed off school for those three days a week was when it struck me most. I thought maybe I could be special, especially if they had made this arrangement, just for me . . .

FIVE

The Bicycle Chain

I earned my first England call-up in November 2000 when I was 14, to play for the Under-15 team in the Victory Shield. The coach was Steve Rutter who decided to play me on the right wing. I told him I was a striker not a winger, but he said I wasn't good enough to play up front. I didn't give him any lip back, but just thought, well, I'd have to get on with it.

The game was against Wales and ended in a 1–1 draw. I didn't actually come on as substitute until the last 30 minutes – and yet was named Man of the Match. Brian Marwood, one of the TV commentators that day, made the award. Brian was later partly responsible for me becoming a Nike athlete.

I came on for Wayne Routledge who was seen at the time as the best of England's Under-15 players. And I agreed, he was excellent. He's now with Tottenham, although he was loaned out to Portsmouth during the 2005/06 season. Also in the England team that day was

Lee Croft, who now plays for Manchester City, although he's not yet a first-team regular. I think those players are the only two, apart from me, who have come through from that England Under-15 squad into the Premiership.

In my next game we played Scotland and I grabbed the opening goal as we won 5–0. In February 2001, I played against Spain and, two months later, against Canada, when I got another goal. In all I played six times for the England Under-15 side.

For three years, I played in Everton's FA Youth Cup side, from the age of 14 to 16. The most exciting period was in the 2001/02 season when we had a very good team. We started off well. I scored twice against West Brom in the fourth round and, in the next, versus Manchester City, I got another two. In the quarter-final, I scored again as we beat Nottingham Forest 2–1 and, in the semi, I twice scored again, this time against Spurs over two legs. So that put us in the Youth Cup Final.

After the two semis against Tottenham, Glenn Hoddle, then Spurs manager, apparently raved about me and asked if I was for sale. Yet again, I knew nothing about that. Liverpool are also supposed to have tried to sign me, having missed out on me the first time.

In theory, I could have gone anywhere. Until signing professional forms, which happens at 17 – although not even that was simple in my case – a lad can still leave and go to any club. But when I got into my 16th year, in 2001, I decided to show my commitment and love for Everton by signing a pre-contract agreement – meaning that, at 17, I would sign the official professional forms with them. It was a way of stopping any other clubs from sniffing around.

I signed during Everton's game with Derby County on 15 December 2001 – and celebrated by going onto the pitch at half-time, in front of 38,000 cheering fans.

Towards the end of that season I travelled with the first team to Southampton as we had quite a few injuries. I was named as sub and sat on the bench. Our fans were shouting for me to come on and I warmed up, right to the last minute, but it didn't happen. I was well choked. In the dressing room afterwards I moaned, saying I should have been used, but only to myself as I didn't really know the first-team players, never having trained with them. But both Alan Stubbs and Gareth Ainsworth agreed and said, yeah, they thought I should have been used, which cheered me up.

Had I come on before the end of that season, I would have been just over 16 and a half and would have beaten Joe Royle's record as the youngest-ever Everton first-team player. In theory, I could have made my debut even earlier, while I was still at school, but that would have been against the football laws; a player can appear in the Premiership when they are only 16 – although not if still at school.

I was due to come on in the next game, David Moyes had told me, and so would still have broken the record, but I was instead picked for the England Under-17 team which was playing in the European Championship finals being held in Denmark in April. I didn't really want to go as I wanted to make my first-team debut for Everton. Everton wanted me to stay and play for them, but an England call-up for a competition has to take precedence, so I had to go. Obviously I was dead proud to play for England, but it was a shame the two things coincided.

In the group stage, we were drawn with Holland, Denmark and Finland. We got through and I scored twice. I then grabbed the only goal of the game against Yugoslavia to put us in the semi-finals in which we were beaten by Switzerland.

There was still another game for us, against Spain who had been favourites to win the cup, in the play-off for third place. Just before it I found I had lost my boots, having left them behind in another stadium. I didn't know what to do. I take size nine and nobody seemed to have a spare pair. In the end, I borrowed a size eight pair from Paul Bracewell whom I knew, of course, from Everton, although on this occasion he was part of the England coaching team. The boots felt a bit tight but they didn't seem to do me any harm as I scored a hat-trick. We won 4–1 and so took the third place award.

The FA Youth Cup Final came right at the end of the season, in the middle of May 2002, and was against

Aston Villa over two legs. The first was at Goodison before 15,000 fans – a huge crowd for a youth game. I scored the first goal after 25 minutes but then got rather carried away. I was convinced we were going to win so, as I celebrated my goal, I pulled up my shirt to reveal a T-shirt on which was written, 'Once a Blue, Always a Blue.'

My cousin, Toni, had done the actual writing. The night before, we'd been mucking around at our house and, as usual, I was saying how much I loved Everton, how I wanted them to win, how I'd always wanted to play for Everton. So we decided to write those words on my T-shirt – and to show it to the crowd if I scored. I've taken some stick for that since, but I don't regret it. I was an Everton fan just like my family.

Bit embarrassing what happened next – we got beaten 4–1. Luke Moore and Stefan Moore were playing for Villa, and did very well.

In the return game, at Villa Park on 18 May, we won 1–0. We should have scored more but their goalie, Wayne Henderson, played a blinder and seemed to save every shot on goal I had, with his hands or legs. So we lost the tie overall 4–2, but I was named Player of the Final. I suppose it was that game, shown live on TV, which gave me some national attention, at least in the football world. It also enabled most Everton supporters, those who didn't normally take much notice of the youth team, to be suddenly aware of me.

After that Youth Cup Final, David Moyes came into the dressing room to see me. Moyesy had taken over from Walter Smith as manager two months earlier, in March 2002. The first team had by then been knocked out of the FA Cup and League Cup and were low down in the League table. Under Walter, they had never finished higher in the League than fourteenth. Moyesy, another Scotsman, who had done a brilliant job at Preston North End, was seen as the best of the new young managers, and all Evertonians had high hopes he would bring us success again.

In the dressing room he told me some good news: I would be training with the first-team squad in the coming season.

There had been calls on local radio stations, during our good run in the FA Youth Cup, for me to be given a proper chance in the first team the next season, to be promoted to the first-team squad and not just sit on the bench for the odd game. I hadn't taken much notice of them.

But now I knew it was going to happen, thanks to David Moyes. I was so excited that I couldn't wait for the summer to be over and to start the new season, which was going to be Everton's centenary.

I played in all the pre-season games, such as at home against Athletic Bilbao. We also went abroad to Austria, and to Scotland to play Hibs. In the Hibs game, I was subbed for fighting. I was just so keyed up, so keen to win and do well. In those pre-season games I managed to score nine goals.

I knew two days beforehand that – at last – I was going to make my first-team debut. It was to be against Spurs, at Goodison, on 17 August 2002. David Moyes told me on the Thursday, but said not to tell anyone.

I didn't except, of course, my mum and dad. On the Friday night, my cousin, James Rooney, was having his 18th birthday party in a local pub, which I'd promised to attend. I went along, but only stayed ten minutes and just sipped a Coke. I didn't tell anyone at the party my news, not even James – it was his do and I didn't want to take away his limelight. I was in bed by ten o'clock but couldn't sleep. When I did, I dreamed about scoring the winning goal – I could visualise it absolutely clearly.

I got up at eight o'clock, but didn't have any breakfast, not even a cup of tea. I didn't feel like anything as my stomach felt a bit funny, although, at about eleven, I had some beans on toast.

My dad drove me to Goodison where I arrived about 1.30pm. When I walked on to the pitch, I could hear the strains of 'Z Cars' playing over the tannoy, and there was a sudden shiver down my spine. I'd heard that tune for years and it always made me feel excited with anticipation. But this was a bit different – the excitement was real.

I'm sure outwardly I didn't look nervous. I'd already

learned to hide my emotion. When you walk out onto a pitch, you want to look serious, as if you're concentrating, so you stare straight ahead.

The wall of noise which greeted me was amazing, so it *was* hard to concentrate. Then I heard the crowd chanting 'Roo-neee, Rooo-nee'.

Kevin Campbell was the main striker that day, with me playing behind him, and I played well enough, nothing startling. However, I laid on our opening goal, passing to Mark Pembridge who scored.

I was taken off in the 77th minute but I don't know why. I didn't want to come off. I was getting a bit of stick from the Spurs defenders who were roughing me up at a corner. Perhaps Moyesy thought I might react, or maybe he took me off so I would get a cheer all to myself – which I did as all the Evertonians knew it was my debut game. The match ended in a 2–2 draw, and I earned good reviews for my own performance.

So at last I had done it, turned out for the Blues first team at the tender age of 16 years and 298 days – only two weeks older than Joe Royle had been. I suppose somebody in the future will break both our records, that's how it goes.

Following the game, I didn't go to the players' lounge. I was too new to know how all that worked, and I didn't really know all the first-team players, not properly.

After my dad had picked me up and taken me home, I just went out into the street to play with my mates, in the normal way on a Saturday evening. Then I went to pick up Coleen.

Yes, just four days earlier, on 13 August after I'd played in a testimonial game at Goodison, I finally managed to get off with her.

I'd been hanging around the chippy after that game with my mates. We'd had chips and gravy, and played a bit of football in the street. The chippy sits at the corner of Carr Lane East, and one of our games was to try to kick the ball and hit a signpost; we also played proper games, and I remember, during the World Cup of 2002, watching Michael Owen score against Brazil – and then running out into the street, pretending to be him.

Suddenly Coleen came past with my cousin, Claire, who was on her bike. Coleen's two brothers, Joe and Anthony, whom I've known for years, were standing with me.

For a long time I'd been saying to them, 'Can you get me a date with Coleen?' They had eventually passed on the message and the reply was that I had to ring her. But I hadn't done so, I was too shy. I also knew she was busy with school work, and singing and dancing in school shows.

As Coleen and Claire passed us, the chain came off the bike. I'm useless with my hands, and have little idea how gears work, but I said, 'I'll do it, Coleen, let me help you.' I somehow managed to fix it and when I had,

I plucked up the courage and said to Coleen, 'Can I have a date?'

She climbed off the bike and gave it to Claire to look after while we went for a little walk round the estate. We just talked and talked, for ages, and somehow got talking about the film, *Grease*, which Coleen said she had the video of, and which I could borrow. So we walked to her house, which wasn't far away, at 37 Carr Lane East – which, of course, I knew well through being friendly with her brothers.

After giving me the video, we went for a walk round the back of our local church, the Queen of Martyrs, and at the back of it we stopped for a kiss.

I then took Coleen back to her house and said good night. She told me she couldn't go out with me the next day, as she had a dance rehearsal at school. But the day after that we went to the pictures to see the Austin Powers film, *The Spy Who Shagged Me*, at the Showcase Cinema on East Lancs Road. I loved it and laughed all the way through, but I don't think Coleen found it as funny as I did.

Later, that coming Saturday evening, after my proper debut in the first team, I arranged to go out again with Coleen. But first, as usual after I got home, I went out into the street and had a kick-around with my mates.

I met Coleen and we went for a walk and then popped into a local pub, where we met my dad and uncle Richie. All four of us just sat around, for about an hour or so, and I had a coke. Later I took Coleen home, gave her a kiss on her doorstep, and went home to bed.

Yes, 13 August is still our anniversary. And I always have to get Coleen a card on that date, or I'm for it.

SIX

A Rose for Coleen

I'd known the McLoughlin family for ages, in fact almost all my life, when I think back. Coleen's dad, Anthony, coached boxing to boys at the Croxteth Sports Club, along with my Uncle Ritchie, so he was my coach as well. They lived locally, and went to the same sort of schools as my family, and we often got invited to their family gatherings. I used to spend half of my childhood playing in Coleen's street, which was better for playing football in than ours.

Coleen was born on 3 April 1986, six months after me. Like me, she's the oldest child of her family. She's got two younger brothers, Joe and Anthony, with whom I played in the street and who were in my gang, although I'm a couple of years older than they are. Coleen also has a younger sister, Rosie, who was adopted about five years ago. Rosie suffers from a disease called Rhetts Syndrome and has to use a wheel-chair. She's a great girl and everyone loves her.

When I was about 10, I remember playing in their street with Coleen's brothers when I got a right telling off from her dad. Joe had run into their house in tears saying I'd broken his brand new tennis racket. He said I'd deliberately smashed it, but I honestly hadn't – it was just an accident. Coleen's dad rushed out and shouted at me, saying I had no respect for other people's property. I didn't give him any lip because I respected him, and I just sort of mumbled that I was sorry. Little did I know how much he would be part of my life later.

Coleen went to St Theresa's RC primary school, the same school as my mum, and later to St John Bosco, a girls' RC comprehensive, and the sister school to De La Salle, just five minutes, walk away.

She comes from a big family, as I do. Her mum, Colette, is the youngest of eight and was a nursery nurse until starting her own family, while her dad, Anthony, is the middle of five, and a bricklayer working for the council.

The McLoughlin family is definitely Irish because they've traced it back and Coleen's dad's grandad came from County Mayo. The year before we started going out the family all went across to Ireland to track down their roots, and found the village that Coleen's great-grandad McLoughlin had come from. Some people living there still remembered the family.

They're a more religious family than ours, I suppose,

at least her dad is. He often goes to church twice a day, visits hospitals, and can give communion to people – I think he's called a Eucharist Minister because he can give the eucharist. Coleen as a child went to church regularly, but at 16 her dad said she could make up her own mind about attending, and he wouldn't force her. She still goes, though not quite as often as she did, and is still religious.

Unlike me, Coleen was always good at school and was popular with both the other girls and the teachers. She says her brother, Joe, is the naturally clever one in their family while she always had to work hard. She's always seemed clever to me, though.

She loved acting, that was her big thing at school. And at her school, the annual play or musical was always a huge event and she was usually the star. She was in *Annie*, *The Sound of Music* and *Calamity Jane*. I heard about them, about how good they were, but, no, I didn't go and watch – I preferred to be out in the street playing football.

Coleen says her earliest memory of me was of being a bit of a pain, probably because of breaking her brother's tennis racket. I was out in the street all the time, hanging around or playing, and she used to hear me talking about my friends. I used to tease them, calling them silly names like the Cat, or pretend to be one of their dads, putting on a funny voice and calling them home. She didn't really like all that; I suppose she thought I was a bit rough, just another kid in the street.

She was a little goodie-goodie, staying in and doing her homework or practising her acting and dancing. One evening a week after school, she went to dancing lessons and one evening to acting lessons. If she did go out, it would just be with other girls, such as my cousin, Claire, and they would sit in each other's bedroom and chat or play records. Exciting, eh?

Coleen claims she never had a proper boyfriend until I came along. And I believe her.

As she had this original image of me as a bit of a pain, she never really thought about me as a possible boyfriend. And I don't think it ever went through her head to think, 'Oooh, he's gorgeous.' I was a mate, someone she had always known about, and a friend of the family. I suppose that's why I could never get a date, I was too familiar to her.

A few weeks before I finally started meeting her, after I'd offered to mend the bike chain, I had at last begun to make more of an impression on her – so she told me later.

She particularly remembers one evening in the chippy. We were both there, but she wasn't taking any notice of me, instead talking to a friend of hers who worked there.

I'd got a mobile phone and was walking up and down the queue, looking at my phone. There was no-one actually on the line, but I knew Coleen would realise it was a hint that I was waiting for a phone call – and a date.

She thought this was funny and started smiling – but, of course, tried not to show it. She didn't say a word but I could see I'd had some effect.

As I was holding my mobile I took off my coat, and underneath I was wearing a yellow Brazil strip, which was a bit tight for me. Coleen thought this was really funny, me walking up and down in a tight Brazil shirt. This time she really started laughing . . .

That was the first occasion, she now tells me, on which she looked at me in a different way and thought she might just fancy me. She thought I had nice eyes and a nice smile – and was funny. No, I don't think she's ever used the word gorgeous, but you can't have everything. There had been lads before me whom she had thought at first sight looked lovely, only to decide they were complete divies.

I didn't know, of course, that I had made much of an impression, so when I met her with the bike I still half expected to be turned down.

The two girls only actually had one bike between them that evening; it was Claire's with Coleen sitting on the back as they went for a ride round the estate.

When we had our kiss behind the church she was in a bit of a panic because she could suddenly see her aunt in the distance coming in her car, and was worried she would see her with me – not because it was me but because her aunt knew Coleen was supposed to be with Claire who was coming to her house for a sleepover. Luckily, she never saw her.

Apparently, when I went with her to her home that evening, I made a rose out of a scrap of paper. I gave it to her little eight-year-old cousin, who was at the door, while Coleen had gone off to find the *Grease* video. It was a rubbish rose, apparently, didn't look at all like one, although I'd told her cousin it was real. But it still amused Coleen.

Over the next few weeks we went out now and again, as it was the school summer holidays, but once school started back she began working hard on her studies, as well as her dancing and acting.

In Coleen's exam results that summer, she achieved eleven GCSEs compared with my total of, er, let me think, none. She got an A+ in Performing Arts, three As in English, RE and Technology, and six Bs and one C. So in September, she went into the sixth form to take A levels in English, Media Studies and Performing Arts.

She had her mind set on going to university. She would have preferred to go to an acting school, in London or the Liverpool Institute for Performing Arts, but had been told the competition for all acting schools was very intense. She was good at acting and dancing, but not so good at singing, so her intention was to take a degree in something like Media Studies, possibly at John Moores University in Liverpool.

In the sixth form, Coleen was still acting in all the shows and became Deputy Head Girl – I told you she was a goodie, goodie – and all despite going out with me.

But in the first few months, it wasn't all that serious. She was so busy and wouldn't go out with me much, at least not as much as I wanted. I suppose she also didn't want to get too involved.

It wasn't until Christmas that we became a little more serious. I bought her a ring from a jewellery shop in the middle of Liverpool. It cost me £2,000 but I'd had some money saved, from an Academy scholarship, and I also borrowed some from my dad.

So by Christmas we were getting on really well. We had a lot in common, the same sort of family and knew the same sort of people, although we don't actually share the same sense of humour. She never laughs at the films or TV comedies I do, such as Austin Powers, *Dumb and Dumber* or *Only Fools and Horses*. She tends to laugh at real people and real things, not people acting.

The fact that I was a footballer, or at least hoping to be one, meant little to her when we started going out. From about the age of 10 she had always known I was mad about football, because I played it all the time in the street. When I'd played for Liverpool Schoolboys – representing the City – she would hear her dad reading the *Liverpool Echo* and saying, 'Oh, there's a reference to Wayne here, scoring another goal.' But she didn't take much notice and didn't understand what being in the Academy meant. It didn't sound like me, being in any sort of Academy – as if I could ever be in some way academic.

Her dad was, and is, a mad-keen Liverpool supporter. If I'd been a Red she might have been more impressed, and I might even have gone out with her earlier than I did. The heroes in her house were Ian Rush, John Barnes and Robbie Fowler, particularly Fowler when he first played for Liverpool and was known by the fans as 'God'. None of the Everton players were ever heroes in their house.

As a little girl she once tried on an Everton shirt which someone had given her. But she only wore it for a day before deciding the colour didn't suit her; she preferred red.

One of her dad's proudest moments, so he's always telling us, was travelling all the way to Rome in 1977 to watch Liverpool win the European Cup Final against Borussia Moenchengladbach 3–1. Dead jammy if you ask me.

As a present for the family, he brought home with him a souvenir, a statue of a horse and chariot. I think it's a symbol of Rome which maybe means something significant and the family has always looked upon it as a lucky symbol.

In fact, when Liverpool won the European Cup for

the fifth time in 2005, me, Coleen and her family were watching the game in her grandparent's pub, with the statue on display on the bar.

FAR LEFT: Me, five days old, October 1985, with my Dad, Big Wayne.

LEFT: Six months old, already a Blue, wanting Everton to win.

BELOW: Aged two, with my brother Graeme, named after Graeme Sharp.

LEFT: I was a lovely smiley baby – and played a good game on the carpet.

BELOW: My second birthday party, and still supporting EFC.

BELOW: Aged ten, school photo from St Swithin RC primary school, with my brothers Graeme (left) and John. I should have worn specs as well but never did.

ABOVE: Taking my first communion, aged nine. I hated wearing the sash and bow tie, and tore them off the moment I left the church, but my Mum still loves the photo.

Wayne Rooney

Did you know that St. Francis built the First christmas crib and the custo continues all over the christian world today?

RIGHT: At school I got excellent marks for RE and my drawing of St Francis was highly praised.

LEFT: My Dad Wayne and Mum Jeannette on their wedding day, 21 March 1987. That's me, 17 months old, in my Dad's arms, looking a bit moany, which is not like me...

ABOVE: Second left, at the back, aged nine, with Copplehouse Boys, the team I was playing for when spotted by Everton and Liverpool.

LEFT: Singing in the school nativity play, aged ten. I still have an excellent voice.

RIGHT: My Dad, Wayne Rooney the first, aged 18 in 1981, winning a boxing cup. As a boy I boxed twice a week, but gave it up for football.

ABOVE: I was Everton's mascot, aged ten, in 1996. Our captain was Dave Watson, while John Barnes was Liverpool's. In the warm-up, being flash, I chipped our goalie Neville Southall.

LEFT: Aged 11, just started at De La Salle comp.

RIGHT: Aged 13, I played for Everton boys at a tournament in Dallas, Texas. I didn't like the food but I loved the rodeo!

ABOVE: The Rooney brothers, me on the right, all hoping to be Everton football stars.

BELOW: Aged 13, feeling knackered, after another hard training session at Everton, hoping that *Coronation Street* won't be long.

SEVEN

Gazza's No 18

I was given Gazza's number. He had just left, so when I joined the first-team squad I was given his number 18 shirt. At Everton, unlike with some clubs, your shirt number, in which you appear on the pitch, is the same as your club number, the one on all your training kit, clothes and such like, so it can be easily found and sorted after being washed.

I wasn't overawed in the dressing room when I got into the first team. There were senior players I didn't know, of course, but I wasn't nervous around them. In fact, I was soon just as loud, and messing around in the dressing room, as I always am.

On the training ground, though, I was perhaps a bit nervous at first, wondering if I could cope at this new level having come from youth football – but that turned out okay as well.

In one of my first training sessions, a ball was played up to me at the front. David Unsworth came to tackle me but I flicked it over his head, ran round him and got the ball. I could hear him shouting, 'You little twat.' I ran on as far as I could, but could hear him behind me, about to clatter me, so I thought the best option was to lay the ball off.

There were no initiation ceremonies, the way there are at some clubs, no-one trying to catch you out or smash into you with their first tackle to put you in your place.

From the beginning, Duncan Ferguson was very friendly. It seemed strange at first, having idolised him for all those years from when I was at primary school. And here I was playing alongside him. Yet, after a few weeks, it felt natural to be training with him.

Duncan thinks that he is still dead young, and can muck around like one of the young lads. I remember having a wrestling match with him when we were involved in a pre-season trip to Austria. Me and one of the youth team players, Kevin McLeod, were in our hotel bedroom playing a golf game on the computer. Fergie said he could do better so my room-mate, who could be a bit of a pest, jumped on him. Fergie soon had him in an iron grip, so I leaped on him to help. We thought we had him, with the two of us on top of him, but Fergie managed to throw us off and pin us down. So that's when I said, 'Okay then, I'll let you off . . .'

The joker in the pack at that time was Mark Pembridge. He had this trick of going round the dressing room when you were away, such as in the physio's room having a massage, and would pick out one item of your clothes which he thought was really horrible – and put it on. He'd then take something from someone else, and put that on and would walk around, wearing all the clothes which he felt were the worst in the dressing room that day. He'd have on one person's shirt, another's trousers, someone's shoes, perhaps a hat – new things in bright colours, in the so-called latest styles, or perhaps old stuff which people always wore and he thought was dead scruffy.

No-one minded, it was just a laugh. Yeah, he often wore a few of my things. I've never been known as a smart dresser, can't be bothered, and, until that stage, I didn't have much money anyway.

Another trick in the Everton dressing room was to watch for someone going to the toilet. If they closed the door and sat down, a bucket of cold water was thrown over the top of the door, all over them. You quickly learned never to close the door. In fact, it could happen at Goodison before an important game, as well as in training, and if you were already in your strip you'd have to get changed.

I once did it to David Moyes – but I ran off and hid as soon as I'd chucked the bucket of water over his door. He never did find out it was me – although I suppose he will now. Sorry Moyesy!

There were one or two 'flash gits' in the squad.

Alessandro Pistone always fancied himself in the latest clothes, and he was always looking in the mirror admiring himself. Gary Naysmith was another one, always fussing over his hair.

Every dressing room also has a moaner. Alan Stubbs could be a right one – and so was I. I still am. I usually moaned about the manager's decision, about the subs he had or had not brought on. When that concerned me I really did moan as I hate being taken off.

I recall once complaining to David Moyes in the dressing room about a training session we had prior to a Saturday game. I said it was too hard for a Friday and we should be doing lighter training.

'When did you become a coach?' he asked me.

'When did you become a manager?' I replied under my breath. I don't think he was able to read my lips.

I once had a row with Alan Irvine, the assistant-manager, during training when he was crossing the ball from the wing for me to head it and score. One ball came over very low, so I volleyed it in and he shouted at me, asking why I hadn't headed it as I was supposed to have done.

'I'd have broken my neck,' I replied, 'trying to head that lousy cross. Cross it properly and I'll head it in . . .'

He didn't say anything to me at the time, as there were other players around, but later he took me aside and said, 'Speak to me again like that, son, and you'll be back in the youth team.'

'No I won't,' I told him, and simply walked off. Not the best way to influence the coaches, I suppose.

My nickname, from the moment I arrived in the first team, was Dog. 'How you doing, Dog?' 'Give the ball to the Dog.' I don't know where it came from. When I was younger, I used to wear an Everton T-shirt which said 'Dogs of War' but I don't think it had anything to do with that. And I can't even remember who first gave me the name; perhaps someone said I looked like a bulldog.

But, from then on, I was known at Everton as the Dog. Only Coleen, my parents and my old mates called me Wayne.

Apart from Fergie, Alan Stubbs and Tony Hibbert were also very kind to me when I first arrived, looking after me and showing me what to do. Stubbsy used to pick me up and drive me home after training, even though it was quite far out of his way. I couldn't drive, of course, and didn't have a car.

David Moyes made it clear from the beginning that I would not be starting every game and I'd be used as a sub. He was trying to protect me, I suppose, in case of something, although. I don't know what. In case I froze, got nervous? Or because I was only 16? No chance. Or in case I wore myself out, wasn't physically strong enough for the Premiership? Unlikely. I considered I could play a full game against anyone, every day of the week.

Or in case I lost my temper? Well, that was a possibility, I suppose. Whatever the reasons, Moyes stuck to his promise of keeping me as a sub, which I totally disagreed with. I believed I was good enough to be playing every game.

He also wouldn't let me do media interviews or appear at press conferences. In doing that, he was trying to protect me from being overexposed, which was fair enough. I hated not playing but didn't really mind not doing interviews; I wasn't keen on publicity anyway, appearing on TV or talking to journalists. I just wanted to play football – and be starting every week.

Straight after my debut against Spurs, Moyes told me I wouldn't be starting the next game against Sunderland. I wasn't happy, but at least he'd made it clear to me. I came on late in that game – as I did for most of the next eight or so – to try and upset the defence. I tried my hardest in the short time I was given, and thought I did well, but didn't actually score.

That elusive first goal came against Wrexham on 2 October 2002 in the League Cup and it was not one goal but two in fact. It made me the youngest scorer in Everton's history at 16 years 342 days. It was a record, so I'm told, that had stood for over 50 years, since Tommy Lawton scored back in 1937 at the age of 17 years 130 days. My dad was dead proud of that.

My first Premiership goal came on 19 October at home to Arsenal. They were on an unbeaten run of 31 games which was incredible. I wasn't brought on until ten minutes before the end for Tomasz Radzinski, and of course by then I was fuming and furious.

I'd only had a couple of touches when the ball was won in the middle of the park by Thomas Gravesen who looped it forward in my direction, although I don't think he meant it as a deliberate pass to me. I brought it down and the Arsenal defence backed off, as if encouraging me to shoot. So I did – from about 30 yards out. It struck the underside of the crossbar and went in. Goal-keeper David Seaman didn't have a chance. I had aimed for the top corner, so I was trying to score, but I didn't know if it would go in. The crowd went wild; my mum and dad were up in the stand and my mum was in tears. In the dressing room afterwards, everyone was cheering and congratulating me – and it was still five days before my 17th birthday.

Afterwards, Arsenal manager, Arsène Wenger, was quoted as saying my goal was 'breathtaking'. He said he thought I was the best English player he'd seen since he arrived in England: 'You don't have to be an expert to see he has a special talent.' That night on *Match of the Day* the commentator remarked when the goal went in: 'Wayne Rooney – remember the name.'

That Arsenal goal made me the youngest player to score a Premiership goal – although, just a few weeks later, James Milner, of Leeds, beat my record.

I gave away my record-breaking boots to Alderhey

Children's Hospital in Liverpool, and they auctioned them off for an appeal. I think they raised a few quid but I don't know who's got them now.

I suppose it was that goal which made most football fans pay attention. But, all the same, I was still not being played from the start which really annoyed me. I told the manager I felt I'd played well when I came on, so what was the problem? Yet he just kept saying I was a young lad and had to be patient.

I scored again at Leeds early in November. I picked the ball up just inside the Leeds half, turned and went past the midfield player marking me. At the edge of the penalty area, I shifted the ball and drilled a shot between Lucas Radebe's legs as he came out to challenge me. It was the first time Everton had beaten Leeds away from home for about 50 years. All my family were there and when I was jumping up and down to celebrate my goal in front of the Everton supporters, I could clearly see my Uncle Eugene in the crowd jumping up and down as well.

I admit I got a bit flash at home against West Brom later that month. We were 1–0 up, thanks to a goal by Radzinski, and when I came on late as sub, as usual, I ran down the line with Darren Moore after me. I suddenly stopped, put my foot on the ball and stood there, hands on my hips, looking him in the eyes as if to say, 'Come on, then, take it off me.' I then burst past him into the box. I might have been taking the mickey a bit, but wasn't playing for time – I was still trying to score. Next day in the papers, Moore was quoted as saying that I had lacked respect. Sorry mate, no disrespect was meant.

Against Birmingham City, at Christmas 2002, I was again brought on as a late sub. I slid in for a tackle on Steve Vickers, the Birmingham defender, a hard tackle, and I came away with the ball. It wasn't a malicious tackle but he got injured and needed eight stitches. Robbie Savage ran to the referee, David Elleray, to protest about my tackle, and I was sent off. I blame Robbie Savage for that as, even after I'd seen the video replay, I didn't think it was a red card offence.

It was the first sending-off of my Premiership career which was only half a season old. Even playing for the youth teams I had never actually been red-carded. I'd already picked up four yellow cards that season, for supposed rash tackles and losing my temper, so I think that counted against me in the referee's mind.

David Moyes defended me. He agreed that it shouldn't have been a red card, and asked the ref to look at the video afterwards, but the red card stood. So as if it hadn't been bad enough getting only ten minutes or so on the pitch as a sub, I was then suspended and had to miss three whole games.

However, at the end of that first half-season in the Premiership, there was some good news when I was voted the BBC's Young Sports Personality of the Year.

I was invited down to London for the awards ceremony and was booked into a posh hotel. I asked Coleen to come with me and she agreed as it was an evening do at the weekend, and she therefore wouldn't miss school. She went with her mum and bought a new dress to wear for the ceremony; she was dead keen to have some new shoes as well, but her mother wouldn't let her buy them, saying they were too expensive at £100. But her mum ultimately relented and Coleen got the shoes after all.

David Moyes, however, blocked Coleen going. I didn't know why and Coleen was very upset. He was going but wouldn't let others go and my parents didn't go to the ceremony either. I don't think David Moyes was right to not let Coleen go, especially as she had made such an effort. Perhaps he didn't want me staying in a hotel with Coleen at my age.

After the ceremony, which was shown live on TV, I received some stick from the newspapers – not on the sports pages but the news pages – for chewing gum and having my tie loose when I was receiving my award. I know my mum didn't like it either and tore into me afterwards when I got home.

It was very hot at the ceremony which was why I loosened my tie. I was hot and sweaty, and if I hadn't been chewing gum I would have singed the presenter Gary Lineker's eyebrows with my breath. I can't even remember who won the main Sports Personality of the Year award, it just passed in a sort of haze.

I don't regret chewing the gum or the loose tie. I was a young footballer getting a prize – for being a young footballer not a fashion model. I'd do the same again; perhaps next time I'll suck a lollipop as well.

I thought the papers went over the top in their condemnation of me and it was my first experience of that. All season they had been building me up, saying what a breath of fresh air this brilliant new young player was, and now they were putting the boot in and portraying me as a young yobbish thug. You can't win.

That season ended with me still coming off the bench for most games in the Premiership – 19 times as sub as opposed to 14 starts. But it was still a brilliant start to my league career league for a lad of my age. The supporters seemed to have taken to me and all my family were thrilled, being such die-hard Evertonians. And so, of course, were Bob Pendleton, the Everton scout who had first spotted me at nine, and the people at the Academy who had seen me progress all the way through.

I can't think of anyone else who joined the School of Excellence at the same time as me who made it into the first team. Anthony Gerrard, Steve's cousin, was in my year and signed professional forms, but didn't play in the first team. The last I heard he was at Walsall. Joseph Jones, the boy I thought was better than me when I first joined Everton, has, I gather, ended up at Macclesfield.

But the bad news for me and my family was that

neither of my brothers, Graeme and John, made it in the end. We were all so disappointed. Everton released each of them when they got to 12. They had been with the club since the age of six, a much younger age than me, and naturally had begun to think they could make it as professionals. I still believe that John, my youngest brother, who's recently been having trials with Bury, might yet come through.

It just shows what a chancey business it can be. You need talent, of course, along with total commitment, and not allow yourself to be distracted. Yes, you need luck with injuries, and with the people who are looking after your career.

I might well have done something silly during the year when I fell out with the coach. I could have left Everton, perhaps even given up football. Good job I didn't.

EIGHT

Agents and Money

I got my first agent when I was aged just 14. I know it sounds daft, and older players won't be able to believe it, but this is what happens today. Clubs are looking at players as young as six years old. By 14 most of the ones that joined have left. A handful do fairly well, but will be destined for the lower divisions. Yet there will always be a very small number, perhaps just two or three, who look likely to become Premiership professionals. In that case, they will eventually be earning a lot of money – so naturally, when they get over 14, the agents start to become interested.

It was my cousin, Thomas Rooney, who was by then playing with Tranmere, who suggested an agent to me. His dad, Ritchie, ran the Croxteth boxing club. He suggested that now I was getting a bit of attention playing for Everton Youth, I should have an agent. He recommended Peter McIntosh.

I didn't have any income of course, not until I was 16

and had left school, but Peter managed to fix me up with an Umbro scholarship agreement. This meant I got £2,000 a year and my kit, such as boots, provided by Umbro. These scholarships have been awarded to several likely young footballers each year, such as Alan Shearer and Michael Owen.

Apart from that, I didn't have much to do with Peter and I never used to ring him which I'm sure annoyed him. But there was nothing much I needed doing for me by an agent at that stage.

It was when we had our good run in the FA Youth Cup in 2002, and beat Manchester City, that everybody seemed to think I would definitely make it to the first team. I then decided I wanted another agent and with my parents I chose to approach Paul Stretford. Mick Docherty, who worked for Paul's agency, Proactive, came to our house to talk to mum and dad who then went to see Paul at his office. I kept out of it, couldn't be bothered with all the business stuff and legal talk. I just slept, curled up on the floor in our front room while they discussed it.

The upshot was that my dad agreed on my behalf that I would be looked after by Proactive. As far as Peter McIntosh went, he was a nice enough guy, but we didn't believe he had the experience we wanted. I was told that anything signed when a lad is still a schoolboy is not legally binding and can be made void at any time. Void, that's the word I was told.

Agents and Money

It all got a bit messy and complicated, with lots of rows and threats in the background. Peter didn't want to give up being my agent, at least not until I had become a full professional. He then sold on his company without us knowing, and I found someone I didn't know looking after me.

I honestly hadn't got a clue what was going on – and it didn't bother me either. I left it to my dad to do what he thought was best. It certainly didn't interfere with my football or distract me from what I really wanted to do – which was to start every game.

Eventually, it seemed to be agreed that Paul would look after any commercial work I had while, for the time being, Peter would take care of my football contract. But I wanted them both to be done by Paul; if I was moving to him, I wanted him to do everything.

It carried on like that until after I'd left school. On joining Everton full time, my pay was £75 a week. Those were my first wages as a player, and all apprentices earned the same. So, really, for the agent there was nothing in it up to the age of 17 when you'd sign full professional forms. They are simply taking a chance, investing in the future. ·

As I got near to signing the professional forms, Everton began to get worried that I might go elsewhere. There were amazing rumours that Real Madrid were after me, as well as Manchester Utd and other English clubs. I never had any interest in signing for anyone but Everton, although I got the feeling that Everton thought the delays were because I was scheming to go for big money elsewhere.

Bill Kenwright, Everton's chairman, took my mum and dad out for a posh dinner to try and figure out what was going on, what my intentions were. They knew I had only ever dreamed about playing for Everton, but the legal arguments were making them suspicious.

Proactive set up a company, with mum and dad as directors, to control my commercial services and which was felt to be one way of getting round some of the complications at the time.

Finally, between the end of December 2002 and February 2003, I agreed a professional contract with Everton – the contract was negotiated by Paul – and, from then on, Paul has looked after everything, the football side as well as any commercial work.

It might look as if all this messing around, involving legal problems and court cases, was the last thing I needed, especially at that age and just starting out. But I honestly wasn't bothered. I just let them sort it all out.

One of the things that Paul fought for when negotiating my first professional contract was my image rights. This is more common now, since David Beckham's time, and it can earn a player more than his football income. I think I was the first-ever 17 year old to have image rights written into his first professional contract which meant I would get a percentage of all commercial rights sold by the club from the start.

Agents and Money

According to the newspapers, my first contract paid me £13,000 a week. Yeah, quite a big jump from £75 a week. My basic salary was, in fact, £8,000, which isn't enormous these days for someone playing in the Premiership – if not quite as young as I was – but with the image rights, signing fees, plus bonuses and other stuff, it probably worked out to more than the reported £13,000 a week.

Paul is still my agent today and I have a two-year contract with his firm. After that, I can leave and go with anybody else I want, but I know if I was unhappy with him he'd let me leave at any time – we have agreed that between us.

I don't pay Paul anything out of my football money, but he receives a percentage of all my commercial work, paid for by my company. Paul looks after everything and I trust him 100 per cent. We've been through a lot together, even in this short time, and I'd be sunk without him. You wouldn't believe the commercial offers and approaches I received, even at the age of 16. There were so many people and firms, most of them trying to rip me off, and use me or my name in some way. I could never have coped without an agent who knew what he was doing and had the experience. How would I have known what to do, which to choose? Mostly it went over my head. So I just let Paul get on with it.

He did, of course, discuss everything of importance

with me first, but I usually agreed, trusting him to protect me from doing too much or being cheated.

At the beginning I used to moan whenever I had any photo shoots to do. I used to say to Paul, 'I'm a footballer, not a model, so why do I have to have my photo taken? Do I really need to do this?' I refused a few of them in the early days, partly because I felt shy and nervous.

Now, I just accept them, take them in my stride. It's part of the business of being a modern player: you have an agent, he has an office and staff who deal with all the calls and requests, and decide what's best for you. If you did it yourself, you'd never have time to play football. So you have to trust them – and I trust Paul's judgement.

Suddenly having a huge income was pretty amazing, but really, I didn't think about it much. I've never really been all that bothered about money and never yearned when I was a kid for material things, apart from sweets. I didn't dream about driving a flash car or having all the latest trendy clothes which are things lots of footballers want.

The first thing I bought, when I started earning proper money was a car – but not for me as I couldn't drive. I bought it for my cousin, Toni, who had helped me write 'Always a Blue'. Toni's a bit older than me and had often driven me to and from training when my mum or dad couldn't make it. I bought her a brand new Mini which cost, I think, £12,500, and I got a real buzz seeing the surprise and pleasure in her eyes.

Not long afterwards I was able to organise for my parents a house of their own, in West Derby – not far away but in a slightly better area. It was a detached house with a nice garden and a big secure gate so they wouldn't get bothered, and was my home as well, of course.

I also bought Coleen some jewellery, such as a necklace and other items, and treated my street mates to meals and other stuff.

I've always got more pleasure out of buying things for other people – especially when they don't expect it – than for myself. I didn't buy much for myself, apart from a better mobile phone and an iPod.

I couldn't drive so at first I didn't buy myself a car. I failed my theory test twice, but passed it at the third attempt, and then sat the driving exam part which I passed first time. I only had three driving lessons.

When I passed my test, and could legally drive, I got a new Ford Ka. It was a sponsored car that Paul and the Proactive team had sorted for me. In fact I got two Kas from them, one a sports version, while later on they gave me a Focus and my dad a Galaxy.

As the money started flooding in, I never thought of going mad and buying a £150,000 Ferrari, which I know many Premiership players have done. I think the most I spent on a car at the time was £45,000 for a BMW X5 which was actually a present for Coleen when she passed her test. I couldn't be seen with it, could I, as I was still sponsored by Ford.

Paul and my financial advisors advised me about what I should do with my money, how I should invest it in things like property. I did think about that, although at first I didn't do very much. When you're young, not married and have no children, you don't think about these things, and you don't see the point of saving. Now, of course, I have a range of investments and a good property portfolio. But back then I just wanted to play football. Getting well paid for it was really an incidental: lovely enough, but not the reason I wanted to be a footballer.

The other incidental, which I hadn't really reckoned on, was all the media attention. It was bad enough when I got into the Everton first team at such a young age, and started doing well. But it was nothing compared with what happened just a few weeks later.

NINE

England

In early February 2003, we were just about to start training at Bellefield when David Moyes called me over. He said he had some news for me.

'You've been called up for England,' he said.

I naturally thought he meant the England Under-21 team. I had played for England Youth, but had never been picked, as yet, for the Under-21s. After all, I'd made only six Premiership starts with Everton, so the Under-21s seemed the best I could expect. And I'd have been well pleased if that was the case.

'Is Hibbo in?' I asked, meaning Tony Hibbert, one of my friends in the Everton team. I hoped he would be turning out for the England Under-21s with me.

'No, Tony's in the Under-21s,' said Moyesy. 'You're in the full England squad.'

I had no idea whether or not Sven Goran Eriksson had ever watched me . No-one had ever mentioned whether or not he'd been in the crowd for any of my games or been checking me out.

I was thrilled, of course, well made up, and dashed home after training to tell my parents. And then I did the usual – went out in the street for a kick-about with my mates.

The England game was a friendly against Australia, on 12 February 2003, to be played at West Ham's ground. The qualifying rounds for Euro 2004, the finals of which would be held in Portugal, had started. England weren't doing very well, according to all the newspapers. They had struggled to draw 2–2 with Macedonia at Southampton. Before that, they had also not been very convincing in a 2–1 win over Slovakia. So everybody seemed to think Sven would need to experiment, bring in new blood, if we were going to win our qualifying group and get to Portugal.

My Uncle Eugene drove me down from Liverpool to meet up with the England team a couple of days before the game. The team was staying at a hotel called the Sopwell House [in St Albans] which was fairly near Arsenal's training ground, because that was where we trained.

It was a long journey and took us forever, and Uncle Eugene wasn't exactly sure of how to get there. But we arrived in time, at 12.30 pm, as we were supposed to. I had lunch with the squad and, afterwards, we all went to our separate rooms. We were told to be back down for a team meeting at three o'clock.

I fell sound asleep, dead to the world. It might have

been the excitement of my first England call-up, or just that I was so tired. We'd left Liverpool really early in the morning. At three o'clock, when I was supposed to be at the meeting, I was still asleep. Someone was sent to get me – but they couldn't wake me up. They had to get a spare key from reception, open my bedroom door, then shake me awake.

Luckily, I didn't actually miss anything as they'd waited for me. It was just an introductory talk by Sven, welcoming the new members to the squad and telling us roughly what was going to happen over the next few days. It wasn't a vital meeting.

There were several players new to the squad, apart from me, such as Franny Jeffers, Paul Konchesky and Jermaine Jenas. But it was weird seeing all the famous players, like Becks, Paul Scholes, Gary Neville, Stevie Gerrard, Frank Lampard and Sol Campbell – people whose faces I knew so well, who were so familiar to me, yet I'd never met them before. Someone like Becks was a role model to me, a person I'd always looked up to. I was a bit nervous, having to walk into a room that first time, in front of 30 strangers.

When we had meals, players tended to sit in little groups – not cliques, really, just friends from one particular club, which is natural. So you'd have the Manchester United players sitting together, with the Liverpool players on another table.

I was lucky in that I knew Franny Jeffers from Everton

and he already knew Stevie Gerrard, though I'd never met him until then. The three of us, all being Scousers, did tend to mess around and sit together, which was good for me. I think Stevie went out of his way to look after me, as a new player, knowing I was from the same background.

David James seemed to be the main joker in the squad and was hyperactive all the time, probably through drinking so many cups of coffee. He was very funny, cracking jokes at the back of the team coach as we went to and from training, and always messing around.

After a day or so, I got used to being with the squad. Watching them on TV from afar, they'd always looked like superheroes. But eating and training with them, I soon realised they were normal people, just like me. I quickly became as noisy in the dressing room as the rest of them.

The training was on a different level to that at Everton – much sharper and quicker. Brian Kidd and Steve McClaren mainly ran the training sessions. Sven just watched, perhaps now and again taking an individual aside to explain something. I liked the look of Sven. He was relaxed and seemed very nice. I was impressed by the fact that he trusted you, as a professional, to do the right thing. He didn't treat you like a kid or an idiot as do some coaches.

We knew before the Australia game that he was going to put out a different team in the second half. The so-called 'first team' would play the first half, then the rest of us would come on for the second. That way, all the newcomers and younger players would get a game of sorts.

Incredibly, Australia were leading 2–0 at half-time. Sven was understandably angry with the first team in the dressing room, so there was a big incentive for those of us coming on to make amends. I played up front with Franny Jeffers – which, of course, was a big thrill for all the people at Everton's Academy who had been coaching us since we were nine years old, seeing us both come on for our England debuts at exactly the same time and in the same game.

I had a long-range shot at goal. Later I might have got a penalty. But I did help create our only goal, scored by Franny. We lost the match, 3–1, but at least we had drawn the second half, 1–1. We made a big thing of this in the dressing room afterwards boasting that we'd done better than the so-called first team.

At just 17 years and 111 days I'd become England's youngest full international player. Apparently, the record stretched back to 1879 when James Prinsep of Clapham Rovers had been capped against Scotland when he was 17 years, 253 days old. I'd even beaten Michael Owen. He was an 'old man' of 18 years and 59 days when he made his England debut against Chile in 1998.

England's next match was a Euro 2004 qualifying

game away against Liechtenstein. We all wondered which of the new players who had appeared in the second half against Australia would get picked, such as Franny and Jermaine Jenas. I made it, though I didn't come on until about 15 minutes before the end, as a substitute for Emile Heskey. We were already winning 2–0 by then. I played quite well and most of the newspapers thought I was England's liveliest player.

Four days later, on 2 April 2003, was the Big One – against Turkey, who were seen as our main rivals in the group. Sven had been quoted as saying it would be 'unfair' to throw me into such an intense game. But I think after my performance against Liechtenstein he changed his mind.

The day before the game, he called me aside and told me I'd be playing, and I would do so from the beginning. Before the game itself, he told me just to play my normal game and enjoy myself. We won 2–0. I didn't score but was named Man of the Match.

I scored my first goal for England against Macedonia in September. It was my sixth cap. We were one down at half-time, not doing well, and, of course, a frantic home crowd was urging on Macedonia.

I'd started up front with Michael Owen. But, at half-time, Sven said he was going to bring on Emile Heskey and play him up front with Michael. I would have to drop back slightly, behind the two strikers. He explained that I was to play at the top of a 'diamond' formation.

I had never played there before, and we hadn't even tried it in the England training sessions. But I didn't mind. I like to think I can play anywhere, in any position and do whatever I am asked to. It doesn't worry me whether I play as a striker or as a midfielder – as long as I play.

Fortunately, the change of tactics worked and I scored in the 53rd minute, latching on to a headed pass from Emile. I was able to hit it first time on the half-volley. I think that actually their goalkeeper should have saved it. So I had a bit of good fortune – and it made me England's youngest-ever scorer.

I got the match ball signed by the whole team, and still have it. Michael Owen wrote, 'That's another of my records you've broken.' Stevie Gerrard scribbled, 'Well done, Ugly Arse . . .'

The really vital game in our qualifying rounds was away against Turkey in October 2003. We needed a point to finish top of the group and therefore avoid the awful agonies of going into the play-offs.

The big story at the time was about Rio Ferdinand, who had been banned by the FA from playing after forgetting to take a random drugs test at Manchester United.

The whole England squad felt it was unfair that he'd been picked on. He was innocent of anything illegal – he'd simply forgotten. I believed him, and still do, because the same thing almost happened to me.

Earlier that season, playing for Everton, my name had come up for a random drugs test. At that time, the club doctor would tell you before training that, afterwards, you were going to be one of those tested.

But when you're training, your mind is totally focused on what you are doing. You forget everything else. So when it finished, I got changed and ready to go home. I was actually at the gates of the training ground when, by chance, I noticed one of the FA officials standing around. Then I remembered: I'd been chosen to have a drugs test. So I stopped and went back. I could easily have left the ground without realising, not remembering what I was supposed to do until much later. And that's what happened to Rio. He clean forgot. My test, of course, was okay. I have nothing to hide when it comes to drugs.

However, just for forgetting, Rio was banned from football for eight months, which we all thought was unfair. He had not committed any offence, had not even been accused of drug taking. Adrian Mutu, the Romanian player with Chelsea, later received only seven months, after he admitted taking cocaine.

So we were all up in arms, led by Gary Neville. There was never a serious threat of us going on strike. None of us ever intended to do that. But we all felt we should take a stand and defend Rio. I didn't really know him all that well at the time. So it wasn't because of friendship. I know the FA have a tough job in monitoring for drugs, and they have an important role to play in ensuring footballers are not abusing the system. In Rio's case, I just felt the FA had been unfair, deciding to make an example of someone. It could have been me, or any one of us.

Since then, they have tightened up the system. It's now very hard to forget to take a drugs test, because officials follow you around all the time. Too much so, I think. It now happens in the middle of training, in the gym, or even on the massage table. The officials hover around, getting in the way when you're trying to concentrate, shoving forms in your face to sign. I think they overdo it now. But I suppose they have a job to do.

The upshot was that Rio couldn't play against Turkey, so we were determined to win it for him.

We played a very disciplined game, with no-one making any mistakes – except for Becks. He missed a penalty. But the match ended 0–0. And that meant we were through to Portugal for the European Championship Finals of 2004.

TEN

Coleen and the Birthday Boy

One of the problems of playing for England at such a young age was all the extra spotlight – not just for me but for Coleen, and even more so because she was still at school. It's probably never before happened that an England international has been going out with a schoolgirl.

I didn't mind getting teased about my girlfriend being still at school, but it made it rotten for Coleen, having all the attention with people trying to photograph and write about her, when all she wanted was to get on with her school work. She missed several of my England games because she was either rehearsing or performing in a school play. She wanted to watch me against Turkey, which was such a big game, but couldn't because she was rehearsing for *Bugsy Malone*, the school production, which was a big event for her.

In September 2003, Coleen had started her second year in the sixth form just as I'd had my sixth game for England and scored my first goal.

Coleen and the Birthday Boy

With Coleen still at school, there were certain things she hadn't been able to do, like join me at La Manga in Spain where we were preparing for the vital final games in qualifying for Euro 2004. All the players' wives and girlfriends had been invited to join the lads for a few days, but Coleen had to fly out a day late, after all the others, due to her school commitments. The press were trying to sneak into her school during rehearsals, to get photos, or would hang around her street and her house, while girls at the school were offered money for stories or photos.

After two weeks of the new term, Coleen decided school wasn't as enjoyable as it once had been, with all the pressure and media attention. The fun had gone out of it and, anyway, quite a few of her closest friends had left in the summer.

The sort of events I was being invited to with Everton or England were usually in the afternoons or evenings, and hard for Coleen to go to. Sometimes she'd liked to have gone with me but it wasn't always possible. So she decided to leave school.

Her teachers tried hard to persuade her to stay, but she'd made up her mind. Her plan, anyway, had been to go to university to do Media Studies or Drama, and later get a job in the media. In fact, Paul Stretford, my agent, was already getting offers for her to do media and fashion work. In one way, it was a handicap for Coleen, being my girlfriend and having all this attention which was disrupting her school life; on the other hand, new possibilities were opening up, because of being my girlfriend, opportunities she was quite interested in pursuing.

She still thinks that one of these days she might go back to college. She earned such good GCSE results that she could get in somewhere if she fancied it, but, so far, she hasn't regretted leaving school when she did.

It was brilliant for me of course, thinking selfishly, because I got more of her time and attention. For a while we lived together at her house, with her parents, and then started looking around for a place of our own.

We became engaged a couple of weeks before my 18th birthday, on 1 October 2003. I'd gone into town and got the ring specially made and designed by a jeweller which cost £13,000. I popped the question on a Monday evening, after we'd watched *Corrie* and *EastEnders*. We were then driving to have a meal at a Chinese restaurant when I had to stop the car in a garage to get some petrol. On the forecourt, I pulled the engagement ring out of my pocket and asked her to marry me. If she'd said no? Well, I'd have put the ring in my pocket and asked her again the next day. But she said yes.

For my birthday itself, I wanted to have a do, as I come from a family which always celebrates important events with a big family get-together; I like getting up, and having a sing and a bit of a dance.

My mum and dad's original idea was to have it in a

pub, in the usual family way, as I still liked to think of myself as a normal person. But when they came to discuss it with Paul, he pointed out all the problems; in a pub, you could not control the guests coming in and out – the paparazzi would have a field day – and there would be endless problems with invites and security.

So, after lots of discussions, we decided to celebrate my 18th at Aintree Racecourse for the benefit of a local Merseyside charity, Alderhey Children's Hospital.

I decided to invite everyone from Everton Football Club – not just the players and their girlfriends but the staff at the training ground, where I'd spent so much time since I was nine, along with their partners. That came to a total of about 60 just from Everton. The only people from the club I didn't invite were David Moyes and Alan Irvine, his assistant, as they were managers. Traditionally, the manager doesn't come to a player's party – it's just not done.

I think perhaps Moyes and Irvine were a bit upset that they were the only ones from Everton not invited. Looking back, it probably helped create some of the problems I had later on.

Apart from all my family, and my best mates I'd grown up with, I also invited a few celebs, such as some stars from *EastEnders* – I've always loved watching it – and I also invited the members of my favourite pop group of the time, Busted.

When news of who had been invited came out and

where the party was being held, there was some criticism in the local paper, particularly from one journalist on the *Liverpool Echo*, and they were saying, 'Who does he think he is?' They were having a go at me for being big-headed, that I was just showing off.

It was made worse when it became known I was selling the rights to details of the party to OK magazine. That really did upset some people, particularly Moyesy, so I was told.

But I think everyone misread what I was doing. We couldn't have held it in a local pub, for security reasons – we knew the tabloids and the mags all wanted to cover it and would somehow have managed to sneak in a photographer or bribed some guests to take photos. It seemed, at the time, the most sensible thing was to let one mag have the exclusive and they would make sure no-one else got in. That was the thinking – but of course it upset the other papers.

What was missed out of many reports was that I didn't make a penny from the party, neither did Paul. All the profits went to Alderhey Children's Hospital, which ended up with a cheque for £46,000, so I did some good for kids less fortunate than me.

One of the sick kids, who has a serious illness, was at the party. I still see him as he has become good friends with Coleen's family. He had a great time at the party and is doing well today.

The food was brilliant. The party organisers had

created a set resembling an American railway station, with loads of different types of restaurant, such as a Chinese and an Italian, plus an English chippy, along the platform. You could eat at each one, or all of them.

I got up and sang an Oasis song, *Champagne Supernova*, which was a good laugh. The song started as a duet with Steve Watson, from Everton's first team, but then one of my old Croxteth mates, John, took the mike and accompanied me. It was great fun.

Then I had a dance-off with James Bourne from Busted. I challenged him to see how long he could dance and I won – I hammered him. It's not that I think I'm a good singer – though I was in the school choir – or a good dancer, it's just that I enjoy doing them. Coleen doesn't quite share my own opinion of my dancing; in fact she usually says, 'For God's sake, don't dance.' So it was a good do, which I enjoyed, and which helped a good cause.

In the summer of 2003, me and Coleen took our first proper foreign holiday together. We flew to Miami and stayed in a hotel for a few days before moving on to Mexico where we'd hired a villa. Both sets of parents joined us. It might seem strange, inviting your parents on holiday when you're with your girlfriend, but we were so young and didn't know what it would be like, just the two of us, away in a foreign place for two weeks.

It was a dead posh villa with staff including a butler

and a chef. One evening we were all sitting in the main lounge when outside, through a glass door, we heard this enormous crash. A terrible storm was going on at the time, so we just thought it was something to do with the bad weather.

Then Coleen's dad suddenly noticed a body outside the glass door – he could see the legs of a body lying splayed out on the floor. We rushed out to find the butler, with all the plates of food lying all around him, who'd slipped on the wet floor and dropped everything. Our first reaction was to laugh as it looked so funny, this uniformed butler lying on the floor and covered in food, but Coleen's dad then realised he was unconscious, having banged his head on the floor. We got him up, brought him to and helped him to recover and he was all right in the end.

During that holiday, we were on the beach one day when Coleen decided to go for a swim but she went out quite far and found herself in rough water. Coleen was quite a good swimmer at junior school, but the current was too strong for her.

When she was about 50 yards out, she started getting into difficulties and began signalling for help. Her dad spotted her waving, but thought she was just being friendly, so he waved back. I suddenly realised, though, that she wasn't waving, but drowning. I raced into the water and swam as fast as I could to reach her. The waves and undercurrent had been so strong that it had even pulled off her bikini bottom. But I managed to bring her back safely to shore. She'd had a terrible fright but I'd saved her life. Our hero . . .

At the end of 2003, Coleen and I eventually found somewhere of our own to live. Paul had been getting us lists from estate agents, but it was Stubbsy [Alan Stubbs] from the Everton team who told us about a house for sale in his road in Formby, not far from the coast. It was newish, quite big with four bedrooms, but nice and secluded. We were both getting fed up with being followed all the time and by this time most of the press realised I was living at Coleen's parents, so it had been hard on them as well as us.

It was good to have our own home at last, instead of living with our parents – which is what most people of our age in Liverpool generally have to do for years and years before they can afford a place of their own, or until their name comes up for a council house. That's what both our parents had done.

We paid just over £1 million for the house, and loved moving in and finally having our own place with our things. It was a dream house, something we'd always hoped we might get one day. So it felt really good – at first.

Then for some reason, I don't really know why, there seemed to be something wrong with it. Perhaps we were too young for such a house, being only 18. But we seemed to rattle around in it. It seemed miles from anywhere, well away from our old haunts and old school mates, and the streets where we'd grown up. We didn't know any people locally, or the district.

It might seem silly but we very quickly got a bit bored. It was probably too big a jump, going straight from an ordinary council house full of people – Coleen's two brothers were still at school – to this fairly big house, all on our own. Although as an investment it certainly proved to be good. We made a tidy profit when we came to sell it after I joined Manchester United. It was my first taste of making a profit from one of my property investments. Looking back, though, we never did feel at home there. Sometimes realising your dream doesn't quite work out.

ELEVEN

Trouble with Moyes

At the beginning of my second season in the Everton first team, in August 2003, we played Glasgow Rangers in a friendly at Ibrox – and I received a really 'warm' welcome from some Rangers supporters. I'd happened to arrive at the ground wearing a crucifix round my neck, and which was, by accident, hanging outside my shirt. I wasn't trying to inflame them, but they certainly gave me some stick as I got off the bus.

Things then got worse. During the first half, I fell and twisted my ankle; it was a pure accident, but it turned out I had damaged my ankle ligaments. I was in agony and, because I couldn't walk properly, the physio drove me back to Liverpool in David Moyes's Mercedes – while Moyesy himself came back with the team on the coach, which was really good of him.

On the way home, I put on a Barry White CD I'd brought with me. Later the next week, though, Moyesy accused me of breaking his CD player, saying it wasn't

127

working any more, and it must have been my fault, trying to shove in my CDs. I think he was joking. I wasn't aware of anything having gone wrong with it and if it had got broken, I hadn't done it on purpose. Must just have been an accident.

I was out injured for three weeks, and it was hellish. I'd never been injured before, not even during my Academy and youth team years. It was horrible, being in the gym on your own doing exercises while all the lads were out training.

I managed to make the first game of the season, coming on late as sub at Arsenal who beat us 2–1. I started in most games that season, unlike the season before, but I didn't start scoring for Everton until December.

It was during this period that I started playing for England, in the European Championship qualifiers, and performed very well. But it led to some club versus country problems which all became a bit complicated and unpleasant.

England had arranged to visit South Africa for a couple of friendly games, but at that particular time I had a knee problem. It was nothing serious, just very sore, but I was taking precautions and wasn't training at Everton.

I knew I wasn't up to playing for Everton, which was what the club had told the FA. But the FA still insisted I should be checked by one of their own England doctors so they wouldn't have to rely on what Everton were telling them. Don't ask me what was going on between them. I was just happy to go for the medical.

Plane tickets were booked for me and Everton's physio, along with Moyesy himself, to see the FA doc in London. By this stage, the England party were at a hotel near Heathrow, waiting to fly off. I still don't know why Moyesy himself needed to come with us – it didn't make sense to me.

When I arrived at the club, I was told we weren't flying after all, but were going down by car with Moyesy driving. This appeared to be a way of avoiding Paul, my agent, who was due to fly down with us on the same plane.

So Moyesy drove us with the physio sat beside him and me in the back listening to my music on my iPod. All the way down I didn't say a word. And when we got to the hotel, we found Paul already there – so they hadn't thrown him off the trail after all.

Gary Lewin, the Arsenal and England physio, and England doctor Leif Sward looked at my knee and agreed that, no, I couldn't play and it had to be rested. So we simply turned round and drove back to Liverpool.

I had known all along that my knee was not up to playing for Everton, or England. I'd told them this and had no intention of turning out for either. So what the hell were they all playing at? I don't know. It looked to me as if Moyes just wanted to be in control. Fair enough, he's the manager, but I thought he had overdone it and it also showed a lack of trust – between the FA and Everton, and both of them and me. All very trivial, but pretty annoying.

It was during that second season that David Moyes pulled me into his office one day and warned me against Duncan Ferguson. 'Stay away from Ferguson,' he ordered. 'He's a bad example to you.'

I immediately told Fergie in the dressing room, in front of everyone – and he roared with laughter. He thought it was a huge joke and started messing around with the lads, saying he was a bad influence and no-one should touch him.

I never, ever thought Fergie was a bad example. His court case, after he thumped somebody, had been a long time ago. He'd been helpful to me from the beginning and I always thought he was a good pro who worked hard, rarely missed training and always ate the right food. I thought he was right for the club, a good presence.

I remember one time when Stubbsy, after I'd moved to Formby and was living near to both him and Fergie, suggested the three of us should visit the pub to watch a Real Madrid–Barcelona game. Fergie, though, said he couldn't go and had things to do at home with his family, so me and Stubbsy went and watched the game on our own. In all my time at Everton I can't remember one occasion when you could accuse Fergie of being unprofessional – in fact he was the opposite.

I think the background to all this was that Moyesy was having his own battle with Fergie. Moyesy took him aside one day, Fergie said, and told him he was now his sixth striker, behind even some of the kids in the reserves, so was unlikely to play for the club again. Fergie suspected Moyes was just trying to get him off the wage bill, but he knuckled down, did extra training – and guess what happened? He did so well, he was later made captain. So God knows what was really going on.

My relationship with David Moyes seemed to go from bad to worse for a period – yet as far as the fans were concerned he was doing brilliantly, not just for Everton but in his handling of me, protecting and doing the best he could for me. He had carefully and cleverly built up the image of 'Mr Everton', the manager of the people's club, and that the good season we'd had the year before had all been due to his management of the players and the club at large.

He even told me after one game which we'd lost – I can't remember against whom – that we'd been beaten because of me and he was now putting me on extra training.

'You've been eating too many f***ing McDonald's!' he screamed at me. I protested that it wasn't true and so why was he saying such things. He just replied, 'I have to treat you differently, because it's you.' I didn't understand any of that.

He made me train on my own for a while and I had to run round Croxteth Park with one of the physios in case I didn't do it properly. I didn't mind the extra training, but getting the physio to make sure I did it properly really annoyed me.

Towards the end of the season, during our away game at Leicester in March, Fergie – who had been named as captain – was dismissed in the first half. As he was walking off, he took off his skipper's armband and handed it to me, and in a purely instinctive reaction I put it on. It certainly didn't intimidate me wearing the captain's armband. I thought I was playing well, and encouraging and shouting at all the other players – doing a sort of captain's role, so it seemed to me.

When I walked in at half-time, Moyesy shouted at me, 'Get that f***ing thing off!' So I pulled off the armband, and threw it on the dressing room table.

I suppose it's funny now, thinking of his fury, and I'm sure it was all heat of the moment stuff, but I didn't consider it amusing at the time. I don't think Fergie had given me the armband to cause trouble; he'd just done so because I happened to be nearest to him as he walked off the field. I certainly didn't put it on to cause trouble. Of course, I realise now that Stubbsy should have had it, as the senior player and vice-captain. So he put it on and wore it for the second half.

I had a few other little rows with Moyesy, and by the end of the season I was beginning to think, 'I can't see this working.'

To me he appeared overbearing, just wanting to control people. Some of the older players thought the same but, of course, they didn't say anything as they were hoping to earn another year's contract. I suppose being young and confident, and playing for England at only 17, I wasn't bothered about upsetting him or answering him back.

Looking back, I'm sure Moyesy was doing what he thought was best for me and the club. I was probably a bit impatient, being so young and inexperienced. But at the time, it bothered me.

The season turned out to be a poor one for not only the club but everyone, for all sorts of reasons. But I always tried my best when I played for Everton – it was still the club I loved and had supported all my life, even though I wasn't seeing eye to eye with the manager.

Everton finished seventeenth in the League that season, just above the drop zone – a big disappointment after all the promise and hopes of the previous season.

Personally, I thought I did much better. In that first season I had been mainly used as a sub, starting only fourteen matches as opposed to coming off the bench nineteen times. That second season I started twenty-six games with eight sub appearances. I also scored nine League goals, three more than the season before, and was the club's highest scorer.

In the April of that 2003/04 season, Coleen reached 18 – and, of course, was planning to have a party. But, at least this time, unlike my 18th, I don't think Moyesy got upset. After all, he couldn't have expected to have been invited to Coleen's – she wasn't playing in his first team.

It was a much more low-key affair than my 18th, without any celebs, and was held in a local hotel, the Devonshire. We invited some of my Everton mates from the first-team squad, but none of the background staff this time.

I did my karaoke bit, singing along to Travis's *Why Does It Always Rain On Me?* My singing was excellent, as always.

The so-called fight that happened probably didn't impress Moyesy, or the club, but it was totally misre-ported. The press claimed there had been a stand-up fight between the Rooneys and Coleen's family, with the police being called and police vans taking people away. That was all rubbish: there was no fight or even any arguments between our families, nothing at all.

All that happened was there was a bit of a set-to – okay, you may call it a fight – between some of my relatives and the bouncers. The bouncers had been trying to clear a floor, move people out of the way, and some of my relatives didn't like the way they were being pushed around. I'm not saying it was their fault, or the boun-cers', but it led to a few punches being thrown and, yes, the police being called.

The papers loved it, even though they got the basic facts all wrong. Not that that makes any difference; once it goes into the cuttings it gets repeated all the time. And so it goes on.

Naturally, my mum and dad were not pleased by all the bad publicity, and neither were Coleen's parents, especially as they are, of course, very sincere church goers.

So what with that, and a poor end to Everton's campaign, I was quite pleased when the season came to an end. Especially as I had quite a lot to look forward to.

TWELVE

Euro 2004

Before the European Championship finals in Portugal in the summer of 2004, the England squad spent a week in Sardinia, to which all the wives and girlfriends were invited. Coleen came and, I think, enjoyed it, except that the weather, for most of the time, was lousy so she couldn't do much sunbathing. The girls, except those who had their children with them, tended to stay up late talking to each other, while most of the lads went to bed early as they had to be up for training the following morning.

Early in June, before we set off to Portugal, we played a couple of friendlies in Manchester, against Japan which finished in a 1–1 draw, and against Iceland whom we thrashed 6–1 with me getting two goals.

France were the favourites to win Euro 2004, but, after them, we were amongst the next countries being tipped to do well. I couldn't wait for it all to start, it was going to be the biggest competition I had ever played in. I was looking forward to playing against Zidane and all the other top players from Europe and, of course, scoring a few goals. I expected us to do really well, as we had so many good players, and I'm sure nobody fancied playing against us.

We stayed at a hotel on the outskirts of Lisbon called the Solplay. I think it was owned by Sol Campbell – that was the running joke anyway. It was a big hotel with good facilities, and lots of space including its own five-a-side football pitch with artificial turf, but, really, there was actually too much room. England had taken over the whole hotel, so no other guests were allowed while we were there, even in the grounds or the bars, and security people milled everywhere.

We were only a party of fifty all together, but there were 119 rooms and the hotel could have held over 200 guests. So there were lots of empty rooms and empty corridors, and we felt a bit lost. As we were spread out, it made it harder just to pop in and out of each other's room, while the massage and kit rooms were on different floors. I suppose it was one of those occasions where the FA bags the best hotel, but it doesn't necessarily turn out to be the most convenient.

I took along my iPod and laptop to watch films or play games on, plus lots of videos and DVD films which I watched in my room, or while having a massage or treatment.

Usually, while having a massage, each player just

listens to their own music on their iPod, so it's all fairly quiet. I insisted on having my favourite films on, though, such as *Oliver* or *Stir Crazy*. I also took *Wedding Crashers*, a comedy, and *One Flew Over the Cuckoo's Nest*.

I watched *Oliver* and sang all the way through while being massaged – well, I do have a good voice, and I know every song. I normally had a massage along with Stevie Gerrard – and he didn't mind. In fact, during the tournament, I tended to mainly knock around with him, Carra [Jamie Carragher] and Michael Owen.

In our group, Group B, we were drawn against France, Switzerland and Croatia. We played France first, on 13 June, in the amazing Stadium of Light in Lisbon. It felt strange to be on the same pitch as their superstars, having watched them for so many years, yet never having met or played against them at international level.

Our aim, going into that game, was not to get beaten, so we were very pleased to go one goal up after 38 minutes when Frank Lampard scored. I later broke away, beating three players before being brought down in the penalty area, but Becks missed the penalty.

When I was taken off in the 75th minute, along with Paul Scholes (Emile Heskey and Owen Hargreaves were brought on in our places), we were still one-up and I thought we'd win.

I didn't protest or sulk, though naturally I would have liked to have stayed on, as I'd half expected it. So far, in my 13 games for England, I'd never played the full 90 minutes.

I assumed Sven's thinking was that by bringing on Hargreaves, we'd defend better and hold on to our lead. I also gathered that Sven was saving me, keeping me fresh for the next game. In that sort of competition, it seems like you hang around for weeks, just waiting, and then, if you progress, the games come thick and fast. You can then face several games in a short space of time, so it's vital to use the full squad, especially as some players need protecting from being overplayed or possible injury. Sven handled it well, he never got bossy, and the players always understood his reasoning.

Anyway, I couldn't believe what then happened. France equalised in the last seconds – and then scored another in the final minute of added-on time. So, from being one-up most of the game, we were beaten 2–1.

Afterwards, there was a horrible feeling in the dressing room and dead silence, which meant we could hear the French lads singing. Their dressing room was right beside ours, and I think their door had been left open – perhaps to let us hear them celebrating. I didn't hate them for singing – we would have done the same – but it was terrible for us, losing at the very end after we knew we'd played so well.

For the next game, against Switzerland, we had to travel to Coimbra, the ancient capital of Portugal, and we spent one night in a different hotel. I can't remember its name, but it was disgraceful; the beds were like prison beds and the fans were allowed into the hotel. We were quite glad it was only for one night.

Before the match, the Switzerland goalie was quoted as saying that I was just a young lad and I wouldn't get anything past him – so that fired me up. And I became even more fired-up when I heard what Tony Adams had been saying on TV – that I shouldn't even start, never mind come on as sub, that I was too young, inexperienced and hot-tempered.

But I did start. And I scored in the 23rd minute – which made me the youngest player to have scored in the European Championship finals. The goal was a header, after a good pass from Michael Owen, and I was so thrilled that I did a backward flip, something I hadn't done since I was a kid playing in the youth tournament in Dallas.

I grabbed a second goal in the 75th minute, after the ball had hit the post and then struck the back of the goalie.

So I was more upset this time at being taken off before the end as I felt I could have scored a hat-trick. All the same, it didn't prevent Tony Adams coming out again with the same old rubbish – that I shouldn't start the next game, even though I'd scored two goals. The only effect his words had on me was to make me laugh.

In our third and final group game, against Croatia, we went a goal down inside five minutes. It could easily have made us panic a bit, but, fortunately, Scholes scored right on half-time. Once again I was taken off before the end. As before, I was really upset, convinced I had a chance of at last scoring my first hat-trick for England, although I took the Man of the Match award as consolation.

We won that game 4–2 and so finished as runners-up in our group, behind France. I was, by then, the leading scorer in the competition, with four goals.

I was well aware of that, as I'm aware of all the facts and figures from my career. I think most players are. I can tell you, looking back at my career, how many goals I've scored in each season. Mind you, it's not been a long career so far. When I get to 36, touch wood, it might then be harder to remember my stats for each of 20 seasons. Or remember anything at all, when I become that old.

We were drawn against Portugal, the hosts, in the quarter-finals. The crowd, of course, was fanatical, but that didn't bother me; I'd played in games with wild crowds already, such as in Turkey.

England went a goal up in three minutes, scored by Michael, and I thought we were doing well and looked like winning. Then, in the 30th minute, I accidently collided with the Portugal defender, Jorge Andrade.

The weird thing was, I didn't feel anything at first. My boot came off and I went after the ball in my stockinged foot. No pain at all. Then I stopped to put my boot back on – and it was hellish. I knew I'd done something awful and signalled to the bench that I had to come off.

I was put straight into an ambulance and taken to the local hospital. As I was wheeled down the corridors, still in my England kit, we went past people watching the match. At the end of most corridors were giant TVs showing the game and, of course, the whole hospital wanted the home nation to win. It was a strange feeling, lying there in my kit, watching their faces as people suddenly turned and recognised me, especially as they had obviously seen what had happened to me on TV a short time earlier.

I was put in a plaster, which didn't take long, and had a needle put up my bum. I couldn't understand that, it'd never happened to me before – I presume it must have been a pain-killer.

The England masseur, Steve Slattery, had accompanied me and we left the hospital to return to the Solplay Hotel in time to watch the end of the game.

I sat at the bar in the empty hotel, with my foot up to rest it, along with Slats. We were then joined by Coleen and Paul, who, when they saw I'd been stretchered off, had left the stadium knowing I would be going to hospital and then back to the hotel.

Portugal, however, had scored in the 83rd minute to make it 1–1, so the game had gone into extra-time. There was another goal each, but no more, and it went to penalties. We lost 6–5 in the shoot-out. Once again the curse of the penalties had struck.

All the players arrived back at the hotel about two hours later. Quite a few stayed up late, with their wives or girlfriends, drowning their sorrows. Sven made no complaints or criticised anyone, insisting we had all tried our best. We were just unlucky.

What would have happened had I not got injured and stayed on? Would I have scored, or got my hat-trick at last? Who knows? I think Darius Vassell, who came on in my place, had a very good game, so I don't think I would have made much difference. The game just went the way it did.

Even though we'd gone out in the quarter-finals, I still ended up as joint-second top scorer in the whole competition, along with Ruud van Nistelrooy. Milan Baros was the top-scorer with six goals. And I was named in the all-star squad of 23 along with three other English players: Lamps, Sol and Ashley Cole.

Sven was quoted as saying how well he thought I'd done, considering it was my first major competition: 'I don't remember anyone making such an impact since Pelé in the World Cup of 1958.' So that was nice.

But I came home feeling a loser. Once again England had been knocked out much earlier than we had expected or thought we deserved. And I came home injured with a broken metatarsal bone in the little toe of my right foot – the same injury Becks famously once had.

When I got back to England I went straight to hospital where the medics examined the foot and gave me a new plaster. They said the old one hadn't been quite right, possibly through being put on too quickly. Probably the Portuguese had all been so busy watching the footie on TV, which was understandable.

I was told I couldn't play for eight weeks – a disappointing end to the competition. I just hoped that in years to come, starting with the World Cup of 2006, I'd get another chance of winning something with England . . .

THIRTEEN

A Scandal Breaks

That summer, after Euro 2004, I jetted off to Barbados on holiday with Coleen. We'd planned it in advance, but of course didn't know when we'd actually be able to go, as that depended on either when England got knocked out, or had won the final. But I had never imagined that I'd end up injured.

I arrived on hols wearing a special air boot in which I wasn't supposed to swim but did so all the same. We stayed at the Sandy Lane Hotel which I thought was brilliant and not at all over the top, as some had suggested. I might have been inhibited by it two or three years earlier, coming straight from Croxteth, but by now, playing for England, I had stayed in quite a few posh hotels all over the world. The staff were lovely as well and we enjoyed our stay.

But when we got home, well, that wasn't quite so enjoyable. In fact, it was the worst period of my whole life so far, for several reasons.

Firstly, for most of the second half of the previous season with Everton, I felt I wasn't getting on with our manager, David Moyes. Then, when talking to all the other England lads in Portugal, I heard about their experiences at their clubs. All the players were getting phone calls from their managers, whilst I hadn't heard from Moyes once – in fact I didn't speak to him until I got back to Bellefield for pre-season training. I became more convinced that if I had a good tournament, and Everton were willing to sell, I would move on. I didn't feel that the club were going to be in a position to win things or move forward and be competitive at the top half of the league.

Then the story broke out about the prostitutes. A newspaper had got hold of something I'd done some years earlier – and, suddenly, it was everywhere, what I was supposed to have or have not done. You can imagine how I felt, not to mention Coleen, and my parents and family, when all this lurid stuff started being printed all over the papers.

Yes, I had been to a brothel, a massage parlour, call it anything you like, when I was just 16. It was not long after I had met Coleen, in those first few months when we were not seriously going out. She had been busy with her school work and school plays. We weren't engaged or anything like that, and, anyway, I didn't know if it would lead anywhere.

I was still going out in the evenings with my old mates,

having a kick-about in the street, hanging around the chippy, the sort of stuff all 16-year-old lads do. On Saturday evenings, they would sometimes go on to a massage parlour and, now and again, I went along with them.

I'm not saying it's okay to do it, or it's justified, it's just what lots of lads have always done – regardless of where they are from – when they go out with their mates and enjoy a few laughs.

I never expected this story from my past to come out – which it wouldn't have, had I been a nobody, just another ordinary lad – and this had happened before me and Coleen had become serious.

But after my success at Euro 2004, the papers were keen to dig up some dirt about me, even if it was years old. They didn't make that clear in the articles, of course – people thought I was still doing such things at that time, or had done so recently.

It's the penalty of fame, I suppose, which you have to live with. People see a chance of making a few quid, if you happen to be well-known, and the papers love it.

As I said, it was all a bit of a laugh, young lads messing around and being flash. Or just being stupid – because, yes, it was stupid to have ever gone to such a place at all, and I deeply regret it.

I was told the night before the story broke that it was going to appear, so I decided at once to confess it all to Coleen. She was, of course, completely shocked and decided to go and stay at her aunt and uncle's place as her mum and dad were away. I made a full confession and admitted I'd made a stupid mistake. Later I went to see Coleen and her parents when they came back from holidays and we tried to talk it through.

What I wasn't aware of at the time was that earlier some girl had told Coleen that I'd once been with a prostitute. Coleen didn't believe it, and felt it was just gossip – or concerned someone who had pretended to be me. That does happen.

For instance, she was in a bar one day with some of her girlfriends when a bloke came up and asked her for a date – and claimed he was Wayne Rooney. Apparently, he did look a bit like me, and presumably went round Liverpool telling girls he was me. Coleen, of course, told him where to go.

Anyway, she'd never told me about what this other girl had said, being convinced it was just malicious gossip. So when I confessed that made it even worse as she had been so trusting and believed in the best of me. She was devastated.

But it was not true she threw her engagement ring into a squirrel compound, as some of the papers said. She was spotted without her ring, so the press put two and two together and made five. It just so happened that she'd left her ring off that day, although I didn't know why.

I felt so ashamed that I'd let her down so much and

brought her all this embarrassment. I've always loved her, and always will, so why had I done such a terrible, shameful thing?

The papers were going wild, following us everywhere and looking for signs of us arguing, anything at all. So we went into hiding. It was a terrible few weeks.

We moved in with Tracey and Shaun, an aunt and uncle of Coleen who were very good, as were her parents. Me and Coleen were not really talking about it much any longer, and she said she could not forgive me. I had nothing else to say except sorry. We didn't know how we would face the future together, or what we would do.

After a few weeks of hiding, Tracey and Shaun told us to sit down and talk it all through, go over what had happened and what it meant. I explained again about being young at the time, just being one of the lads, and not knowing how serious the relationship with Coleen was going to be.

They told us we had to move on, not sit in silence or mope. So we started going out a little bit together, to places like Blackpool and Manchester, so as to get away from Croxteth and all the gossiping, or the press trying to photograph us.

I am sure parts of the press were trying to split us up in order to keep the story running. We both realised that and decided we didn't want that to happen. We didn't want to let them win and get what they wanted. I can honestly say both Coleen and I will always be grateful for the kindness and support Tracey and Shaun showed us.

For a long time afterwards, Coleen lost her confidence. And it was all my fault. She is naturally very bubbly, loves going out, meeting people and social occasions. She'd enjoyed doing the little fashion events and media things she had begun to be offered. Now she didn't want to face anybody – the public or even people she knew. It was a very difficult period.

But both our families were a great help. They stuck by us, helped talk us through it. Eventually Coleen felt strong enough to go out and face people without feeling ashamed, embarrassed or worried about what they might be thinking or saying behind her back.

It all still comes up of course; newspapers continue to drag out the same old stories, and probably will do for ever.

Coleen knows that by taking part in all the press and media events she now does, and being interviewed on TV, she is making herself a target. By putting herself in the spotlight, people will have a go at her and repeat the same old stuff. That's the penalty, because of my actions, we both have to pay.

It's my biggest single regret in life. I can never sufficiently make it up to Coleen – but I have tried, and am trying . . .

All this gave Coleen a quick lesson in what the press can be like when you are in the limelight. They love building you up, and love just as much kicking you when they think you are down.

What all of this taught me is that whether we like it or not, both Coleen and I are in the public eye. We are being watched everywhere and there is always someone looking to make an easy buck.

Every time I got in the car, I was looking in the mirror to see if I was being followed. Even with close friends and family we both had to mind our lips.

The most harmless little comments, if passed on, can be twisted and turned into a story. And it's awful when that happens because it means you can't be open and honest with your family and friends. You have to protect them as they often don't realise what the press can do with even the most trivial piece of information.

While all this continued to rumble on, my future at Everton was in question. Should I stay or should I go?

FOURTEEN

'I Don't Want to Play for You Ever Again'

It's hard to explain why my relationship with David Moyes began to go wrong. When I first got into the Everton team, and did so well in my first season, everything seemed to be fine. I never felt any jealousy from any of the players in the Everton dressing room. But, the next season, I began to think there was one person who seemed to be a bit upset and envious of what was happening to me – and that was Moyes. He must have had his reasons but never said anything to me.

I suppose he had expected to get most of the attention himself following that good season when Everton had ended seventh, by far our best position for six seasons. But when he realised I was getting so much of the limelight I felt he resented it. That's how it seemed to me.

On the other hand, I could be wrong. He would say, as manager, he was simply doing the right thing in trying to take the press and public attention off me, to help me settle into the team in peace and quiet. But at the time I

ABOVE: Aged 16, signing a pre-contract with Everton – Dad and Mum are behind, with Walter Smith, the manager.

BELOW: No, it wasn't my 40th, but my Dad's, in 2003. But, yes, it is my wonderful, gorgeous, talented and clever fiancée Coleen.

LEFT: Our council house at Armill Road, Croxteth, where we lived until I was about 11. I played football in the street every day, even when I'd signed pro forms for Everton.

RIGHT: In my bedroom window, I showed which team I supported. My Dad gave me the Everton number plate on my first birthday – he still has it, in the front window of his house.

LEFT: De La Salle comprehensive, where I gave no trouble, won a few bob in the playground in a game called 'Jingle', got good school reports, but left at 16 with no GCSEs.

ABOVE: 19 October 2002, five days before my 17th birthday, celebrating a goal against Arsenal to become the youngest Premiership scorer.

BELOW: Signing for Everton in January 2003, with manager David Moyes. A happy day, but later I wasn't so happy with Mr Moyes...

MAIN PICTURE: Euro 2004, Portugal. My first big tournament with England. I did well, and so did England, until things went wrong…

OPPOSITE, TOP TO BOTTOM: England 3, Switzerland 0. I got two goals. The first one, a header, made me the youngest player, at the age of 18, to score in the European finals.

England 4, Croatia 2. I bagged another two goals – and then got taken off, much to my fury.

England vs Portugal in the quarter-finals. We were a goal up after three minutes, then I went down in the 30th minute. My metatarsal had gone. I was out – and so were England, beaten on penalties.

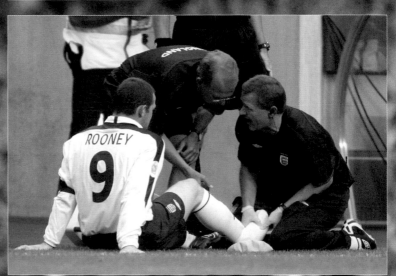

ABOVE: In August 2004, I signed for Manchester United, and Sir Alex Ferguson.

BELOW: I made my United debut in September against Fenerbaçhe, scoring a hat-trick.

LEFT: Man Utd vs Newcastle, April 2005, my best goal so far. I was angry with the ref, and took it out on the ball.

BELOW: Smartly dressed, as ever, for the PFA Young Footballer of the Year award in 2005, which I also won in 2006.

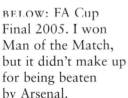

BELOW: FA Cup Final 2005. I won Man of the Match, but it didn't make up for being beaten by Arsenal.

Helping Coleen lay the foundations for a new £2 million wing at Clare House Children's Hospital which her sister Rosie attends. But for football, I'd probably be digging holes full time…

While visiting the hospital, I got a surprise birthday present.

didn't see it that way. As I said, he never took the time to explain.

For example, he wouldn't let me do any post-match interviews or appear at press conferences. Fair enough. But there did come a time when I would have liked to have had my say – such as after that red card against Birmingham City. I'd wanted to explain the tackle wasn't malicious, just hard, and I hadn't gone in to hurt anyone. I would have liked to have given my point of view but wasn't allowed to.

And yet, when I signed my professional contract, the club called a huge press conference to announce the news and present me to the media. I was staggered when I walked into the room. There were over a hundred press people and twelve different TV crews. It was a nightmare. I had no experience of such things, of course, so I wondered why he was making me do it. Then I realised: it was good publicity for Everton – and for Moyesy himself, having signed me.

I sat beside him at the table, and in front of me was a big bottle of water and a couple of little glasses. I took a swig from the bottle of water, picking it up and holding it to my mouth. I could hear Moyesy whispering beside me, 'Use the f***ing glass!' I just ignored him as I couldn't understand how I was doing anything wrong; that's how I normally drink from a bottle of water. I didn't see why I should change my habits just because I was in front of all these people.

Today, I can see his point. I don't always think quite like that. I have become more aware that footballers are seen, whether they like it or not, as role models. So I don't deliberately do things which young kids might copy without thinking about it first. Then, of course, I still might do it . . .

Anyway, this was my first press conference and I didn't want to appear phoney, just myself.

Just before the press conference began, someone must have realised how young I was, how it could be a big ordeal for me, especially when they discovered just how many press people were going to turn up. So, at the last minute, they decided to drag in Tony Hibbert as he'd just signed his new contract.

Tony told me later that he was in the pub, having had a few pints, when he got the call, and was told they wanted him to come quickly to help me out.

He arrived and sat at the other end of the big table opposite me. Tony was introduced and it was explained he was signing a contract with Everton as well. But all the focus was on me and he only got asked about one question.

I really don't like the press attention, having to answer their questions. I just want to enjoy myself, playing football, that's all. But I now know it's an important part of being a professional footballer, so I have to learn how to handle it.

*   *   *

'I Don't Want to Play for You Ever Again'

The attention after Euro 2004 was much greater than it had been when I'd been playing for Everton. And I have to admit we made one big mistake in handling the press.

When Coleen and I went off for our holiday in Barbados, we knew we'd be followed everywhere.

In the hope that we'd get them off our backs and let us enjoy our hols in peace, we decided to do a deal with News International covering both the *News of the World* and *The Sun*. We decided to tell our side of the story because people had started selling untrue stories about us.

What a terrible mistake. We'd forgotten that the people of Liverpool hate *The Sun*, for what the paper printed after the 1989 Hillsborough tragedy, criticising the Liverpool crowds. *The Sun* has never been forgiven for that.

In Liverpool, that was all brought up once more – and *The Sun* had to apologise once again – something which I think they blamed me for. So they still appeared to have it in for me, despite having got their exclusive.

The deal had done no good at all, and we regretted it. Paul, my agent, took the blame, but I felt at fault, too, having thought it was a good idea.

I was only 18 at the time, and still learning. A lot of players sign exclusive newspaper deals and now, on reflection, I'm not sure it's the right thing to do. In my opinion, the paper you sign with only looks after you for as long as you're with them. The others feel they don't get any access to you, so they love to stick the boot in – it's a no-win situation.

Anyway, with all this going on, I made up my mind to leave, if possible, in the coming transfer window. I explained my feelings to David Moyes.

He asked why I wanted to leave. I didn't rubbish him but just said it was for personal reasons: all the crap in the paper about the prostitutes had been getting me down, and I just wanted to get away from Liverpool.

The next day it was in the *Echo*, all the stuff about the prostitutes making me feel fed up. I was absolutely furious as I'd been talking to Moyes in private. I couldn't see how the *Echo* had got the story without some sort of leak from someone. So next day at the training ground, in front of all the players in the dressing room, I had a real go at him.

'You expect me to sign for a manager I can't trust? I stormed. 'How did that story get out, except from you? You're a f***ing joke. I don't want to play for you ever again.'

I was really worked up and probably said things that a player should never say to a manager, particularly not in front of all his team-mates. I was also pissed off because the club made it look as though it was just me who wanted to leave, but it wasn't true. Whilst I had been with England in Portugal for Euro 2004, chairman Bill Kenwright had given an exclusive to the *News of the World* saying it would take £50 million to prise me away from Everton. The club had also sent Trevor Birch, the new chief executive, to Portugal to meet Paul, my agent, to discuss the possibility of me leaving and asked if I was prepared to go to Chelsea.

As I still had three years left on my contract, Everton would be able to sell me for good money. They'd got me for nothing, after all, so they'd do very well financially.

Some days later, Moyes asked me if I wanted to go to Liverpool, as they'd apparently shown interest. I told him he must be joking, that as an Evertonian born-and-bred, how could I go there? I didn't feel I was deserting Everton but just getting away from Liverpool, the problems and David Moyes.

I never heard from Chelsea about their supposed interest, and neither did Paul. During August, there were endless rumours: one Sunday newspaper said that Newcastle United were offering £30 million for me which I didn't believe for one minute – although it did seem to be true when they made an official bid of £20 million.

If no-one else had come in before the transfer deadline was up I would have gone to Newcastle. But, in truth, I would have gone almost anywhere just to get away from Liverpool and David Moyes.

A few days later, Manchester United came in, offering the same sort of money as Newcastle. The minute they appeared, I knew that was the club I wanted to join. I had never felt anything against Manchester, or United, despite having grown up in Liverpool. I never saw them as a hated rival, but instead as an excellent club which had won loads of pots, and would, I expected, win lots more. I wanted to win things with them.

By now, I was training again, recovering from my metatarsal injury. I wanted to train hard but Everton became worried that I'd break down and be injured again. They wanted me to take it easy as they were desperate to get top money for me. A price of £25 million plus add-ons was put on my head.

The fans, of course, didn't know about my strained relationship with Moyes, and still don't to this day. At the first Everton home game, they again shouted my name, but this time sung, *'There's only one greedy bastard.'* They also seemed to forget that, at the same time, there was speculation about Board changes and the need to bring money into the club. As far as I'm aware, the only significant money brought in was my transfer fee. So what would have happened to the club if I hadn't left?

It was a terrible six weeks. During this period there was the prostitutes story and, for most of that time, I didn't know where my future lay. Plus, I was trying to recover from my foot injury.

When news finally came out that I could be leaving for Manchester Utd, our house at Formby was covered in paint and graffiti with people spraying things like 'Munich 58' and 'Judas' in huge letters on our walls. It was unbelievable.

I remember once sitting at Coleen's uncle's house, watching TV with Coleen. Viewers were texting in slagging me off, and saying I was a rat to leave Everton, that I was never a 'true blue', a right greedy bastard, a selfish hypocrite, and all that.

So I texted a message of my own: 'I left because the club was doing my head in – Wayne Rooney.'

The Sky presenter then made an announcement: 'Would the people pretending to be Wayne Rooney stop sending text messages.'

Later on, though, I think they realised it must have been me, because they made a strange reference to me watching the programme:

'We know Wayne Rooney is watching – and we are watching him.'

We began to wonder for a moment if someone had a secret camera outside. We were sitting in the conservatory, without curtains or blinds, and it was all dark outside so you couldn't see who might be there. For a moment it was a bit scary, as we thought someone might really be stalking us . . .

What did become truly scary was the level of threats against myself. Even Paul was receiving countless death threats. In the end, I was becoming desperate to get away. I'd had enough with the prostitutes story and now the transfer saga. The attention had all been too much, and we were also fed up with our Formby house.

Newcastle upped their offer, but it was rejected by

the Everton board. Then Manchester United offered more. Sir Alex Ferguson, apparently, had hoped to wait until the January transfer window to buy me, as he had already spent so much that season. But he somehow managed to get the money from his next budget and was able to spend it ahead. So, on the last day of August, before the transfer window had closed, the deal was done. Manchester United agreed to pay Everton £30 million, made up of guaranteed payments and perform-ance-related bonuses, and the contract was signed on 30 August 2004. Until I signed the contract I'd never met Sir Alex before as all the negotiations had been done between Everton and United, with Paul looking after my interests.

There was a last-minute hitch when the release papers weren't signed by Everton. Then they dropped the bombshell that they would not allow the transfer to go through unless I agreed to waive my remaining signing fee. It was unbelievable. I cost them nothing, they had got the best part of £30 million for me after two years in the first team, and they wanted to have my signing fee.

Later on, another side issue was my parents' house, the one they had moved into in West Derby in 2003 after I had signed professional forms for Everton. Paul had negotiated that the club provide a house near the training ground for me and my family to live in until I'd got engaged to Coleen and we'd eventually moved into our own home in Formby.

'I Don't Want to Play for You Ever Again'

After signing with Everton, the club bought the house and paid the mortgage. Had I stayed until July 2006, the house would then have become my parents' property. By leaving early, I had to buy the house from the club and pay them back what they had paid for it. Nothing needed to be done until July 2006, but Everton had other ideas and tried to force me to pay early or have my parents removed from the property. Needless to say, they didn't win that one.

I probably would still have left Everton eventually, even if I'd got on well with Moyes.

I think I would have stayed at least one more year, that had been my original plan. My heart had always been with Everton and it had always been my dream to play for them. But all players are ambitious, they have to be. And when it comes down to it, however much they might love their club, they have to put their own career first.

I thought that by going to Manchester Utd I would do better as a player and win more trophies. I can honestly say that Old Trafford has been everything I dreamt it would be, and there's no doubt I made the right decision to join the club.

FIFTEEN

The Boss and Man Utd

I was surprised by how tall Sir Alex Ferguson was. Usually famous people, even footballers, turn out to be smaller than they originally appeared. The day I signed for Manchester Utd was the first time I'd ever met him.

He took me to the training ground, which was empty, just to show me around and explain the layout. I was well impressed. It was much bigger, better and newer than Everton's training ground, with more pitches and a bigger gym.

Next morning, I arrived for training. I was given the number 8 shirt, my squad number, and the one vacated by Nicky Butt. In the dressing room I went round and shook everyone's hand. No-one took me round or introduced me, I just did it. I wasn't nervous as I had been two years ago, on my first day in Everton's first-team dressing room. I already knew quite a few of the Manchester Utd players from the England squad, such as Rio, Scholesy, Wes Brown and the Nevilles.

I didn't know Roy Keane who was clearly the boss man, the leader. But there was no real initiation stuff, except just one: new players are smashed down three times in training, just to show them what it will be like. That didn't happen to me, because I arrived still injured and only came into first-team training very slowly, so they all knew I had to be careful.

For the first month I was mostly working on my own, one-to-one with the physios, in the gym or running. I wasn't allowed to do any contact work or any work on the ball. So I was pretty bored and frustrated.

It was made worse by living in a hotel, the Alderley Edge. I felt trapped. There was nothing wrong with the hotel, which was fine, it was just living in such a place I found horrible. Coleen was with me and she didn't like it either, so we started looking around for something as soon as we could, either to rent or to buy.

Gary Neville tried to persuade me to buy one of his houses. I don't know how many he has, or whether he was boasting or winding me up, but he kept telling me about these properties he had. In the end, at the end of that first month when I was finally ready to play, we moved into a rented house in Wilmslow. We agreed to take it for six months, to get us up to Christmas, by which time we hoped we would have found something of our own we liked. By the time I came to make my United debut, we were at least settled in a house, even if we didn't own it.

I thought I was ready and raring to go a good week or so before Fergie decided I was. I kept saying to him, 'Pick me, boss, pick me,' but he just said I had to be patient.

I was doing full training by then with all the lads and I found it much easier than it had been at Everton. I always thought that Everton trained us too hard; sometimes I was knackered by the time we got to Saturday. At Manchester Utd, the sessions are shorter, sharper, and more enjoyable. The boss and the coaches treat you with more respect and seem to trust players more than Everton had.

In pre-season training, there are always two sessions, one in the morning then another in the afternoon. At Everton, we would start the second one at 1.30pm, straight after lunch before you'd even digested your meal, and then work until three o'clock. At Manchester Utd, we would rest after lunch, then do another session from 3 to 4pm. I thought that was much more sensible.

Three days beforehand, the boss took me aside and said I would be playing against Fenerbahçe. This was to be on 28 September 2004 in the European Cup, at home. That would make it ninety-six days since I had last played a game, back in Euro 2004 when I broke the bone in my foot.

We were drawn in Group D, along with Lyons, Fenerbahçe and Sparta Prague. United had already played away at Lyons in the first match while I was injured, and drew 2–2.

I scored my first goal for Manchester Utd after 17 minutes when Ruud van Nistelrooy put me through and I beat the goalie with my left foot. Ten minutes later, I netted a second. Ryan Giggs rolled the ball to me, I dummied a defender, and scored with a low shot from just outside the box.

Just after half-time, we were awarded a free-kick on the edge of the penalty area. Normally, Giggsy or Ronaldo would have taken it. With Ronaldo off the pitch, Giggsy shaped up to take it – but I grabbed the ball and told him, 'I'm taking this, I want my hat-trick.' 'Go on, then, take it,' he said. I did, and sent it curling into the top corner.

At the end of the game, I swapped my shirt with one of the Fenerbahçe players – I think it was Aurelia, the Brazilian. I wasn't really concentrating; I was more inter-ested in getting the ball and ran after the ref who was carrying it off the pitch, but I couldn't make myself understood. I told him I'd scored a hat-trick so the ball was mine. He just kept on walking.

In the dressing room, the boss must have heard me moaning so he went off to see the ref and came back with the ball which I got all the United players to sign.

Obviously it was not the ball I had scored all three goals with – at least I doubted if it was, although I suppose it could have been. In the modern game, different balls come on and go off the pitch all the time. But, tra-ditionally, the ball the game finishes with counts as the match ball. I still have that ball, safe in my trophy cabinet at home. The cabinet is actually in Coleen's room, the one she calls her office, as I don't have such a room.

As for the shirt, the one I gave away, it was, in fact, the one in which I scored my third goal. I changed my shirt at half-time, as we always do because it's nice to put on fresh kit if you've got all sweaty, wet or dirty. That shirt, in which I'd scored the first two goals, now sits in the Manchester Utd museum, although it still belongs to me.

Everyone was shouting, cheering and joking with me in the dressing room, but I didn't stay long. Coleen and I went back home, to our rented house, where I had a glass of Cloudy Bay, a wine from New Zealand. It's a white wine that Coleen buys a lot.

My next game was my Premiership debut for Manchester Utd, but it didn't go as well. It was against Middlesbrough, at home the following week, and ended in a 1–1 draw. I didn't play very well, I don't know why, but it just happens. Perhaps I had been running on adrenaline in that first game, perhaps being out of football for those 96 days had eventually caught up with me, I don't know. You are trying just as hard, doing all the usual things, but some passes go astray for some reason, or your first touch is not perfect. All you have to do then, until your touch comes back, is concentrate on giving easy balls.

I scored my first league goal for United in October,

against Arsenal at Old Trafford. This game became notorious as the 'Battle of the Buffet' and, from the very beginning, the atmosphere was pretty tense and nasty, although nothing to do with me.

There had been a history between Manchester Utd and Arsenal. For about eight years they had been neck and neck, taking it in turns to win the Premiership title. Everybody expected one of them to win it again – although by then José Mourinho had arrived at Chelsea ready to spend some of owner Roman Abramovich's billions. But Arsenal had still managed to win the title the previous season, despite all the Russian's money, and they came to Old Trafford unbeaten in forty-nine games, which was incredible.

About 15 minutes before the end, I was brought down in the penalty area after being tackled by Sol Campbell. The Arsenal players went mad, insisting I had dived which I hadn't done, while Ashley Cole and Campbell rushed up to me and accused me of not having been touched. I agreed with them. I hadn't been fouled; I'd just gone down because of my momentum as Campbell stopped me. But we were given the penalty, which was lucky for us. Ruud scored, which made them even more furious. I then scored a second goal in the last minute to finish Arsenal off.

As we came off the pitch there was a lot of jostling. The Arsenal lads seemed to be most worked up about Ruud, accusing him of cheating. There had been a bust-up between him and Patrick Vieira in a previous game which had lingered on.

I was in the dressing room, taking off my shirt, when I heard shouting outside in the corridor. I went out and a scuffle was taking place between some of our players and the Arsenal team. Everyone was shouting and pushing and yelling. Perhaps a few haymakers were thrown as well, although nothing serious. An Arsenal player threw a piece of pizza at Sir Alex. It must have been lying around, left over from a buffet, and it hit Sir Alex and made a right mess of his suit jacket. I thought whoever did that showed a great lack of respect to a manager who has done so much for the game.

I then piled in, looking for a piece of the action, preferably with Lauren. He was right in the thick of it and seemed to be causing all the trouble, after making sarcastic remarks throughout the game. I tried to get at him, but was pulled off. Eventually, though, the security men broke it all up and we filed back into our dressing rooms.

Afterwards, the boss had to change his suit, because it was in such a mess, before he could do any interviews. But the battle itself was nothing really, just handbags at five paces with a bit of pizza thrown in. Nobody got hurt, except maybe the kitchen staff, who obviously felt the pizza was good enough to eat.

I had a fairly poor disciplinary record that season – seventeen yellow cards in all. Against Bolton on Boxing

Day, I was fouled by Tal Ben-Haim who also gave me a mouthful, so I gave him a push. He went down like a bag of shite, as if I'd knocked him for six with an upper-cut. I wasn't sent off at the time, but I received a suspension afterwards when the video evidence was studied.

Then, in an England friendly against Spain, Sven took me off before half-time – apparently to save me from myself before I was sent off. I wasn't pleased – I knew I would be coming off at half-time anyway, as that had been the plan, so I thought he could have left me on until then.

Spain had been taking the mickey, passing the ball back and forth, and showboating which upset me. When that happens, you have to try and break up your opponents' passing game by getting stuck into them, tackling hard and quickly. Perhaps I overdid it because I was so frustrated, but we couldn't get a kick of the ball. Not nice.

I like to think that today I've calmed down a bit. I'm still likely to get a yellow card for a mistimed tackle, which can happen to anyone, or for going in a bit too hard. But I've put a stop to offences like dissent and kicking the ball away, those really stupid things for which I used to get a yellow card. It was daft, getting suspended for three games just for arguing with the ref.

Losing my temper, though, well I'm sure that will still happen. All players do that at some time. In the heat of the game, you can get carried away and swear and shout,

169

which is something I rarely do off the pitch and never did at home as my mother would have slapped me. But it's like being at work on a building site or whatever, it's the language that's used.

Now, because of who I am these days, TV cameras will often show a close-up of me swearing, which they don't do so much to the other players. It's given me a reputation for effing and blinding on the pitch more than most, which I don't think is fair.

In that first season, I was carrying on with Roy Keane, even though I had just arrived in the team. If I had made a mistake he'd give me a mouthful, which I expected him, as the captain, to do, but I would also give him a mouthful back if I thought he hadn't played the right ball. Afterwards in the dressing room, though, it's all forgotten.

I thought personally that I had a good first season, but it wasn't really so good for the team, not when Manchester Utd set such high standards.

In the 2004/05 European Champions League, we got through from our group into the last sixteen, but were then beaten 2–0 by AC Milan over two legs. We had our chances, but never took them; in fact, in the second match Giggsy nearly scored and, had he done so, I'm sure we would have gone on to win the tie.

We reached the FA Cup Final in which we met Arsenal once again. I thought we dominated the game but once more didn't take our chances. The game went to extra-time and penalties, and unfortunately we lost. To this day, I don't believe Arsenal deserved to win, but that's what happens when you're not clinical in front of goal. I received the Man of the Match award, but it didn't make up for not getting a winners' medal. So we finished the season without a trophy, which was very unusual for Manchester Utd.

I started twenty-four games, plus five as sub, and I finished as United's top scorer in the Premiership with eleven goals. I also got three in Europe and three in the FA Cup, making it seventeen goals altogether which I was pleased with. I was also elected the PFA's Young Foot-baller of the Year, voted for by my fellow professionals.

In my three seasons so far in the Premiership, I had increased my goals tally every season. So I decided that would be my aim every year from now on: to do better each season.

Obviously, that can't go on for ever – but I can try. Let me see: in another fifteen years, if I keep up this rate of progress, I should be averaging about 200 goals a season. Now that is something worth aiming for . . .

SIXTEEN

Personal

We found our dream house at about Christmas-time that first season, but we didn't move in until many months later as it had to be built, or at least rebuilt. We fell in love with the whole situation. The land was in a very quiet part of Cheshire, near a golf course (though I don't play golf), and a retirement home for old folks – and though I'm not old or retired I will be one day, so it will come in handy.

On the land was a smallish white house, an old one – at least it looked old to me – and there was already planning permission granted for it to be knocked down and a new one built. We went along with the design, which had all been agreed, and took on the plans of the architect and designer although we added a few ideas of our own.

It has, let me think, six bedrooms and a big kitchen which is very modern and greyish – I'm not good at describing decor. Running off the kitchen is a big conservatory where I usually loll on a couch and watch TV. We also have an indoor swimming pool along with a games room which hasn't been finished yet. The garden covers about two acres.

There are no live-in staff, just me and Coleen, but we have a cleaner and a gardener who each come in once a week or so. We have a state-of-the-art security system and a big gate and fence, so no-one can see our house or garden. I had enough trouble when I lived at home with my mum and dad when we had so many fans as well as supporters of rival clubs hanging around, and at our first house at Formby when we suffered all the vandalism.

So we were determined, when we moved in, that we would never allow any press or TV into our home, even if *OK* or whoever offered us millions. One positive thing about having had early success was that we learned our lessons quickly: you can't moan about wanting privacy if you then let photographers into your lovely house. And it is lovely – not lavish or flash, the way it was described by some papers, the ones which called it 'Waynesor Castle' (as opposed to 'Beckingham Palace'); it's quite modest and not too different from the other houses around us.

Often, if Coleen is away, I won't stay there. I get a bit lonely on my own, so I'll spend the night at Coleen's parents and stay in the extension they have had built. They still live in the same house on the same estate they always did, but they eventually bought their home from the council, as did my mum and dad before they moved.

Despite having moved into their own house, my mum still enjoys her work at my old school as a dinner lady and earns about £287 a month, insisting that she doesn't want to live off her son.

Coleen is doing plenty of work these days, and isn't scared any more to go out in public. She has a column in a magazine, *Closer*, is writing a fashion book, and does photo shoots and modelling. She also has a contract with Asda to promote George clothing. I'm all for her doing this stuff.

She does appear to have quite a few holidays compared to me, but I encourage that – in fact, it's often me who suggests it. I can't get time off during the season, and with either the European Championships or the World Cup coming round every two years, it means that even the close-season gets shorter and shorter. I can't expect her to wait eleven months every year before she can have a holiday, can I? She's an outgoing girl, after all, who likes to have fun.

So she heads off with friends, which usually includes my cousin, Claire, who is still one of her best mates, or perhaps her parents. And I totally trust her, despite what some of the tabloids have tried to stir up.

Once she was in Tenerife with her friends when one paper managed to get a photo of her dancing with a barman. It was in the hotel they were staying at and lots of people were doing a sort of conga dance in a circle and holding hands. But, because the photo was cropped so carefully, the rest of the people weren't seen – and it was the moment the picture was taken that Coleen happened to be holding hands with the barman.

On that trip, one paper bribed a young man to follow Coleen down the street and, at a certain moment, run up and kiss her. It was a total set-up, just to make it look as if she was going out with some lad. She rang me, upset and furious, to warn me about the picture, and decided after that to come home from her holiday two days early because she couldn't stand being harrassed and insulted any more.

The press also try to make out Coleen blows a fortune every week on shopping, and that I give her £100,000 a month to spend, which is rubbish, especially as she now earns her own money and doesn't need mine. She's just a normal young girl who likes shopping and who just happens to have more money than most other girls of her age – but she doesn't spend all her time doing it.

These stories all began when Coleen visited New York a couple of years ago with her aunt and uncle, and six other relations. Naturally they had a lot of luggage and shopping bags. Coleen got pulled up in customs due to excess luggage.

We have an equal relationship, neither one of us is the

boss, and I don't expect Coleen to wait on me hand and foot. I know about the old image of a footballer, that he had a little wife waiting for him to come home from training, and she would then get out his slippers and dab his brow; she never went anywhere or did anything on her own.

In most modern relationships, not just those in football, that doesn't happen any more. Coleen has a career of her own which is good and I'm proud of what she's made of herself. She's had to put up with a lot being with me.

One of these days we will have children, but Coleen says she would prefer to be married before starting a family. That is her religious belief, and I respect that.

We have our rows, our ups and downs, like most normal couples – which is what I think we are despite having a lot more money than most people, and, of course, a lot more pressures and attention than they do.

It is difficult to do 'ordinary' things, like going to the pub or even Asda. Even if we manage to avoid the press, there's always someone who claims he's an Everton fan and wants to insult me, or someone who hates Manchester Utd and wants to have a go. Or someone who thinks that, because I look 'hard' on the pitch, I'm hard in real life, and so wants a fight to prove how tough he is. Strangers were always having a go at Roy Keane, and often he reacted. People say obscene and terrible things and it's hard not to respond, but I've learnt to stay calm.

Steve, my bodyguard, usually responds for me and keeps them away.

It's awful having to be careful what you say even to family and friends. Something may sound harmless or trivial, but if it gets passed on it can become exaggerated and taken out of context, and then some paper will build it up into a story.

As a person, I am fairly laid back and I don't get upset easily or take offence. I laugh at most things that are said about me, however horrible, and don't mind being called 'potato face' or Shrek.

When Stevie Gerrard called me 'ugly arse' I wasn't upset. It didn't actually mean I am ugly or have a face like an arse; it's a common Liverpool term of endearment which you use about your friends.

I've never worried about my looks, even as a young teenager when I first started going out with girls. I never thought I was handsome but didn't think I was ugly either; I just always thought I looked, well, normal.

I suppose that's because I'm not vain. I am not fussed either way about my appearance, and certainly don't spend any time looking at myself in the mirror.

Perhaps the only thing I used to worry about was my hair. When I was about 16 I began to think my hair was receding which concerned me – after all, no bloke wants to lose his hair. I still think about it from time to time and although it probably is thinning I don't really worry that much.

As for hairstyle, I've never gone in for one. How I look is how I've always looked as far as I can remember, just as my mum first brushed it I suppose. What's the point in worrying about it? I just want to look like me, just ordinary. The only thing I ever do with my hair is to have it short – that's about as far as any style goes. I may let it grow for a few weeks but then have it shaved back. And the only reason I would let it grow is laziness, not because I particularly want it to be longer. Coleen always gets on at me to have it shaved as she hates it long. But I keep putting it off because it doesn't really interest me. When I do have it cut, either Coleen or her mum cuts it; I just can't be bothered to go out to a hair salon.

I don't care much about clothes, either. I get some stick in the Manchester Utd dressing room because I regularly usually turn up in slippers. I have two pairs, just soft ordinary carpet slippers, with one pair from Marks & Spencer and the other just a cheap pair with an England flag on the front bought from the market.

I wear slippers when driving to training in my car as they're so comfortable. After all I'm going to work, and you don't need to be smart when it's just football training held in private. I don't understand those players – and there are quite a few – who turn up in the latest fashions or the trendiest casuals every day. I don't know where they get the interest or energy.

The United players have a go at me, and call me a

scruff, but I always have a go back. On one occasion, Edwin van der Sar turned up wearing a blazer and designer jeans. A blazer! I thought that was funny as I don't call that relaxed gear for going to work in.

I live most days in old jeans, a jumper and trainers, unless I have to go somewhere in public in which case I might make a bit of an effort – although not always. What's the point? I just want to remain me. So each day I tend just to put on what's handy or lying about.

People think I look just like one of the fans, going to the match and wearing what they wear, as opposed to a well-known footballer, but I want to look like an ordinary supporter.

I do have quite a few suits but only really wear them on certain occasions and events.

About twice a year I might buy some new stuff. I usually go to a place called Flannels in Manchester and buy some new jackets, a coat, a suit or whatever. I will probably spend a few grand, then that's it for another six months or so. I'd never think of window shopping and looking at the latest styles.

There was once a story in the papers about me and Alan Stubbs, when I was at Everton and we were playing away at Chelsea. The article said we filled in time on the morning of the match by going into an estate agents on the King's Road. The estate agent apparently couldn't understand a word we were saying, and was suspicious about our scruffy appearance, so, thinking we were 'scally' burglars looking for houses to break into and not realising we were footballers, he rang the police.

It was quite funny, I suppose, but total rubbish. I have never been in an estate agent's in my life. Right from the first time I was thinking of buying a house, I got my agent, Paul, or someone from the office to get lists of houses and check them out.

I do have a few tattoos, which I suppose could make me look like a cartoon version of a burglar. The first one I got, at a place called Quiggins, in the middle of Liverpool, was not long after I met Coleen. It's just a little one, at the top of my right arm where it joins my shoulder, and naturally says 'Coleen'.

Later, I went into a tattoo place I happened to be passing with one of my mates and had the word 'THEN' tattooed on my back, just above my bum. He got the word 'OK' tattooed in the same place. It was just a joke between us; we were always saying to each other, 'Okay, then?' So we decided to take one word each and I chose 'THEN'.

After Euro 2004, I had tattooed below my Coleen tattoo a big sort of Celtic or Irish cross, but I'm not sure of its exact name. I might get another one at some stage.

Just to finish off the body matters, I have six fillings in my teeth – all those sweets I ate as a kid, I suppose.

I own a pair of specs which, when I remember, I wear for driving or watching TV, but I can see well enough without them. The club has suggested getting contact lenses but, because of the lazy right eye I had as a child, it would be hard to fit them. But it doesn't worry me on the pitch, my sight is good. When the ball comes to me, I'm always thinking rather than looking, working out what I'm going to do next.

Some football experts have said, I have unusually good vision, as if it's my eyesight that's amazing, letting me see round corners. Or I must have a swivel head. I don't think it's either. It's more to do with painting a picture. Before a ball comes to me, I'll look up quickly, taking in where everyone is, then I won't look up again. I'll then pass immediately but almost instinctively, reckoning on where people will now be. It's done at great speed of course, so you have to have a good eye-to-brain connection. It's come with training over the years, with knowing the players I'm playing with and what they might do.

One thing I have developed a passion for is cars. Since my sponsored Ford Ka we have had a few but nothing too extravagant. A couple of BMW X5s, a Mercedes Jeep and a Mercedes SLK. When Coleen started earning decent money she bought herself a new Range Rover, and just before the England squad left for Germany in 2006 she bought me an Aston Martin Vanquish as a surprise early birthday present.

Financial advisors look after all my investments, and put my money into sensible things. I don't really bother about those things much, and just trust them to do it. I know I've got three apartments in Florida and a villa in Marbella along with other property developers in the UK but I haven't seen any of them, just the photographs.

A few months ago, I bought Coleen another engagement ring. The original ring was quite old and we fancied having something newer and better, so I bought her one full of diamonds. It cost a packet and I certainly couldn't afford it when I was at Everton, but she deserves it for putting up with me. I don't know the style or exactly what sort of diamonds they are, but it's a pretty big ring. When Coleen's going out to ordinary places she usually wears the old ring while the big one she keeps locked up only to be worn on really special occasions.

Okay, I realise that doesn't make us sound like an ordinary couple, being able to spend that sort of money on one ring, but, all the same, we still think we are . . .

My idea of a good night in is a typical Monday night – when I can watch *Coronation Street*, *EastEnders*, the second lot of *Corrie* and then catch the second half of the live football on Sky. A good night out would be a meal around seven o'clock with Coleen and her family, either in a restaurant or at her house when her mum will either make something of fish or chicken, or we'll order a takeaway, and later all go for a drink at the pub.

If I had to pick three words to describe myself, I'd say 'romantic', 'funny' and 'hard'. I like to think I'm romantic. When Coleen turned 18, I placed an advert in the birthdays section of the *Liverpool Echo*. It read, 'Coleen McLoughlin – My Babe is 18. Happy Birthday. Love Always, Wayne xxx.'

It's the sort of thing I would have done anyway, even if we had been an unknown couple. The ad was cheap enough, only £60, but I thought it was romantic, sincere and funny. I also spent £4,000 on a gold bracelet for her.

People often laugh these days when I give my name. If I have to ring Sky, for example, because the TV is on the blink, or when I'm on the phone ordering something by mail order, they always burst out laughing when I come to give my name. 'Oh yeah,' they say, 'pull the other.' They think it's a wind-up, that I'm not who I claim to be. It's often very hard to persuade them, so I have to go through endless security checks, such as dates of birth and stuff.

Yes, it is quite funny being Wayne Rooney.

SEVENTEEN

Inside the Dressing Room

On an ordinary training day I set my alarm clock for 7.15am. I've never really slept in, so I don't need it, but I still put it on, just in case. I only shave about twice a week, but not on any particular day, as I hate it, can't be bothered. I don't tend to have anything to eat or drink. And, no, I don't take Coleen a cup of tea or coffee in bed – although I would if she asked for it – as she doesn't drink either of them.

I leave the house at about 8.30am and drive the thirty-minute journey to United's training ground. Coleen is often still in bed when I leave, unless she has to get up for a job. The players are not due for training until ten o'clock, but I like to be early. I'm usually there around nine and often the first one to arrive along with Gary Neville. The boss is usually already there, working away in his office, but we don't see him.

I get changed into my training kit and a pair of old trainers, and leave my stuff in my locker. No-one locks their locker – I don't think anyone would want to nick my clothes anyway.

Then it's upstairs to the canteen for some tea and toast, and a chat to Gary, some of the coaching staff, then with the other players when they arrive. Most come to the canteen first for a cup of tea or coffee.

I might pick up and glance at any newspaper lying around, although not very often. I don't read newspapers, and never have done. We don't get a newspaper delivered at home, and never did when I lived in Croxteth – we're not a newspaper family. I get my news, such as it is, from the TV, mainly Sky Sports as I don't really follow world affairs.

The first thing we do, when training begins, is visit the gym and get on the bikes. We do fifteen minutes each, just to relax our legs and warm us up, before getting our boots on and going outside to the training pitches.

We always start with box work – passing the ball back and forth across a square patch about twenty metres wide, not much bigger than a large living room. Eight players stand outside the box with two inside; the two inside – it always starts with the two youngest which usually means me and Ronny (Cristiano Ronaldo) or Giuseppe Rossi if he's in our group – wear bibs.

The object of the exercise is for those outside to pass the ball back and forth across the box to each other while the two in the middle try to intercept it. When one of those in the middle gets the ball he takes off his bib and replaces the player on the outside who has given away the ball. It's all good fun and I enjoy it.

That lasts for not much more than fifteen minutes. We used to do it for far longer at Everton but, as I said, at Manchester Utd all the exercises are shorter and quicker.

We then work on tactics for about thirty minutes in the form of heading, shooting or crossing. There may be special tactics used in relation to the game coming up, because the coaches want us to try something ourselves or be aware of something the opposition might do. I don't find this as much fun because you often have to stand around while the coaches plan certain moves or make you repeat things over and over. Sir Alex doesn't take the training as such although he obviously knows about everything going on. Carlos Queiroz, his assistant-manager who lives and breathes tactics, does so instead.

After all that, we'll have a practice game, which is what I like best, usually across half the pitch, and ten versus ten. Carlos or one of the other coaches picks the teams. Players normally play in their usual positions, although occasionally they may play elsewhere just for a change. I often go in goal towards the end of the game. I love playing in goal, but then I love playing anywhere really. Nike featured me in a World Cup advert playing in goal.

Training tends to last two hours and most players

finish off by going into the gym to do some body work, especially if they have a slight injury problem.

I never work on weights – I don't need to. Perhaps it was the years I put in at the boxing club as a lad, or just the way I'm built. I have a natural strength in my upper body so don't need to work on my muscles as most young players do. If I ever found myself getting knocked off the ball then I'd do some weights training, but I have been fortunate with my build.

Normally, during the season, I weigh 80–82 kg, which is about 12 st 10 lb–13 st. I think that's best for my build and my height, which is five feet ten inches. Most players these days are taller and lighter, like greyhounds, but I'm more of a bulldog, as everyone is always telling me.

At Everton, I was made to do a lot more gym work and hard training, and the club liked me to be 12 st 3 lb, but I was never happy with that and felt drained before every game. I'm happier with my present weight, so is the club and so is England. I look upon it as my fighting weight.

In the close season I usually put on half a stone. It's not through overindulging in fast food, ice creams or soft drinks, it's just through not training. So I have to work hard to get it off when we restart after the close season has ended.

I think I eat sensibly enough – the club never worries or tells me off. I naturally like pasta and chicken, which is what the club usually tells you to eat, not steaks or fast food. But I do have a sweet tooth and take two spoonfuls of sugar in tea, although sugar does give you energy.

I have lunch at the training ground, like most players, and eat chicken or pasta.

I love going to training. I enjoy the work and banter with the lads and staff, and I've never found it a burden or a bore. I don't like the gym work so much, or the endless tactics, but I love anything on the pitch and working with a ball.

In a typical week, perhaps for half the afternoons, I might have an engagement, so, after training, I will drive myself there or may get driven if it's in the middle of Manchester or London. The Proactive office has a car with a chauffeur which me and Coleen use. The driver is Shaka Hislop's brother, Kona, who was once a pro himself for Carlisle United. He helps us in other ways, too. Proactive also have a security man, or bodyguard if you like, called Steve who's an ex-police detective sergeant. When I'm at public events, he's there in the background, just in case someone wants to pick a fight or hassle me. Unfortunately, it happens.

Perhaps one afternoon a week I have to do promotional work for my sponsors which, at the moment, include Nike, Coca-Cola, EA Sports and Asda. Me and Coleen are the so-called faces of Asda, who use our photographs in promotions, so I may have to attend a photoshoot or the launch of a new product. It doesn't take long, two hours at most, and the events tend to be held in Manchester, so it's handy.

I sometimes have a business meeting as well, which is usually held in my agent Paul's office in Wilmslow, which isn't far away. If it's to meet the lawyers or accountants, they will tell me what's going on and I try hard to understand, but in the end I leave things like investments and finances to them.

About one afternoon a week I will also do some charity work – for Alderhey Hospital or Claire House Children's Hospice, where Coleen's sister, Rosie, attends, or maybe another children's charity. That normally involves having photographs taken, going round the wards, meeting kids and signing things. I don't mind any of that – I like to think I can help kids less fortunate than myself.

If there's nothing on at all, then I'll come home straight from training, which means I'm back by two o'clock. Otherwise, if I do have something on, then I'll get back about four.

All I do then is rest. I just lie on the couch with my feet up and the TV on. I can stay like that for an hour, two hours, all evening, in fact, if Coleen is away, and I often fall asleep while lying there. I'm brilliant at doing absolutely nothing.

It might sound as if I'm dead lazy, a bit of a dosser. Which is probably true. Most footballers are physically lazy except when it comes to performing: they'll take the car to the local shop, don't like gardening, avoid any physical jobs and just loll around most afternoons. But, don't forget, we've been doing hard physical training all morning, so, after all that, you need to rest.

Virtually all professional sportspeople go through the same routine every day – train, eat, rest. That's what their lives consist of. And, of course, the club wants you to stick to that – not to be rushing around, getting exhausted and putting yourself under any sort of physical or mental strain.

Perhaps, when I get older, I may take up golf, which is what many players enjoy in the afternoons. Some also have a little business of their own which they can go and play with. At the moment, though, I don't do any of that.

When I first joined Manchester Utd, I was caught out with a few tricks in the dressing room. For instance, a ball would be lying on the floor nearby, so you'd attempt to kick it – but it would be on a string and someone would pull it away just as you were about to hit it. Ha, ha, ha. Or you'd go to pick up a water bottle and someone would suddenly pull it away; that, too, would be on a string. Just the usual type of childish practical jokes.

At United, unlike Everton, there's been nothing as bad as throwing a bucket of cold water over someone as they sat on the lav. But the lads take the same sort of mickey out of your clothes if they think you're wearing something awful or outrageous. The worst that really happens is that you'll find your clothes hanging up from the dressing room ceiling.

When I first joined, Ronny and Quinton Fortune were the main jokers, always playing tricks which I thought were quite funny.

We have the different sorts of characters you get in most dressing rooms. People tend to get slotted into certain roles, and always get the mickey taken for the same sort of things – for being mean, slow, vain or whatever.

People ask me all the time who I have preferred playing with – Ruud van Nistelrooy, or Louis Saha. I like playing with both of them, as they have different strengths. Ruud holds the ball so well, is good at link-up play, and scoring. Louis looks to go behind their defence which gives us more space. But I don't have a favourite.

In this last season just finished, Ruud and Ronny have supposedly been falling out and Ruud has been sulking. I haven't been aware of it. People argue all the time in training. Ruud's a good lad. I've never found him moody. I've learned a lot from him, but of course as the main striker, you can get depressed if you're not scoring.

People say Ronny overdoes it, doing too many step-overs. Perhaps he does now and again, but that's him expressing himself, which I think is good. In fact, I think he's brilliant. But he's still young, still learning.

Carlos Queiroz, the assistant manager, is the main coach. He's a good coach, but you wouldn't want go to out and have tea with him. He lives football. He moans a lot, but then that's his job. That's what coaches do – moan at you.

Fergie, of course, is The Boss, no question. You wouldn't want to get on the wrong side of him. He wants you to do the right thing for yourself, and for the team. If you don't, that's it. I've heard all the tales about what happened in the past. When I arrived he gave me a few one-to-one talks, just advice on things like money, how to invest wisely.

The best trainer at the club, when he's fit, is Paul Scholes. His shooting and passing is incredible. You try to be on his side in a training game as you know you'll win. As for those looked upon as the worst trainers, Wes Brown is usually a bit stiff as well as me, I suppose. I've certainly got a reputation for not liking certain things, such as gym work.

Rio also thinks he's dead skilful, always wanting to come forward and show off his amazing abilities, or so he believes. He thinks he's really playing number 10 in the Brazil national team. I'm always taking the mickey out of him.

The hard man? Well, that's me, isn't it? I always play to win whatever the game. I suppose the hardest tackler is Wes Brown, you don't want to be tackled by him in training. As for the quickest players in the squad, I'd say Ronny, Louis Saha, Mikael Silvestre and Rio.

The worst dresser, at least the one we most take the

mickey out of, is Louis. You should see some of his track suits. Ugh! Darren Fletcher gets the mickey taken for doing stupid things, on and off the pitch, but mostly he's a great lad.

Longest time in the shower? Rio and Louis, who can take for hours – working on their lovely hair, I suppose.

The biggest moaner is usually me. I will even moan afterwards if we've been beaten in a training game, blaming everyone and saying how unfair it all was.

In that first season at the players' Christmas party, one of the youth team dressed up as me. He wore a number 8 shirt with Rooney on the back – and he also sported a Shrek mask. Shrek's the cartoon figure whom I'm supposed to resemble, but I didn't mind, and laughed along with everyone else. It's a Christmas party tradition at United that the young players take the mickey out of the first team.

I began wearing black gloves after I'd joined Manchester Utd whenever it's really cold. I don't know why as I never did so at Everton. Perhaps I saw one or two others, like Ronny and Giggsy, doing so and copied them. I met Graeme Souness one day at an event and he mocked me, saying how surprised he was that a hard man on the pitch like me should wear gloves, and was I going soft?

As for nicknames, amongst the Manchester Utd players, I'm known as 'Wazza'. Nobody now calls me

'Dog', as I was known at Everton. Only Coleen, along with my and her parents, call me Wayne. I don't know who in the United dressing room first called me Wazza, or why. It could be after Gazza, but I don't know.

On match days, when we're at home for a three o'clock or an even later kick-off, the players have to be at Old Trafford three hours before the start. On such occasions, I usually have a long lie-in, then drive myself to the ground to be there for 12 noon. On arrival, someone always parks your car for you.

We then have a meal together. I always have the same thing – spaghetti bolognese with a piece of chicken fillet. I don't have any pudding, not before a match, and drink water and perhaps a cup of coffee.

Afterwards, in the players' lounge, short videos of our opponents, highlighting their main set-pieces, will be shown, and the coaches will go through them. The final team meeting will take place in the dressing room. The Boss – which is what we call Sir Alex, not The Gaffer – will read out the team sheet although we will all pretty much know by then what the team will be because of what we've done in training.

If someone isn't playing, The Boss will already have taken them aside before this final meeting and told them. It happened to me about twice last season, once against Blackburn. Sir Alex told me I wasn't being dropped but rested as I'd been playing too many games. I protested, because I always want to play, but I didn't moan and sulk. You have to accept that The Boss is usually always spot on.

In this final team talk, Sir Alex will go over their main players. If we're playing Chelsea, for example, he'll warn us about someone like Didier Drogba. Then he'll go over both their set-pieces and ours. Giggsy always takes our corners, and he and Ronny our free-kicks.

The Boss will also discuss how to defend at corners – something which is written up on the wall. One of the coaches, such as Mike Phelan, will have written, with a marking pen on A3 sheets of paper, our opponents' team sheet as soon as we've received it so we know who we're playing against.

Our main defending players will be earmarked to mark each of their main players when they take a corner. For example, Rio, Nemanja Vidic and Gary Neville will be told they will be picking up Drogba, John Terry and William Gallas, although it depends, of course, on their team.

My positioning at corners is always the same – I stand at the edge of the box and mark the man who will be nearest to that position which, in the case of Chelsea, is usually Joe Cole.

This team meeting only lasts about fifteen minutes as Sir Alex is only really going over stuff we already know.

If there's time, we'll sit around the players' lounge,

messing about and watching the TV. Family and friends are not allowed in there until after the game. Finally, we'll go to the dressing room and get ready.

If it's an early kick-off, and we're at home, we have to arrive at Old Trafford at 6pm the previous evening. We then climb aboard the team coach for the trip to the Radisson Hotel in the middle of Manchester. There we have a meal together and I'll eat the usual – although as it's the night before a game I may also have a pudding as well, such as chocolate pudding and custard. They certainly do a good one at the Radisson.

After the meal, we retire to our rooms – each person has their own room – and just watch TV or muck around. Some of the lads might visit each other's room and play computer games or just chat. Nobody will have a drink or go to the bar as it's forbidden. Sometimes The Boss doesn't mind if a friend or relation, or a business contact, comes and chats in the hotel for an hour just to pass the time. But if it's a big game, it's banned – he doesn't want us being distracted by out-siders coming into the hotel. We have to be in our room by 8.30pm, resting or sleeping. I usually watch a film or two and then get to sleep by about 12.

Next morning, we'll get to the stadium three hours before kick-off, and go through the usual routine.

For away games, we will train in the normal way the day before at our training ground, from 12 noon, and the next day we'll leave for wherever we are playing in enough time to be at the ground at least one hour before kick-off.

Last season, we started to travel to away games by train. All teams used to do that in the past but, for the last thirty years or so, most professional clubs have used big luxury coaches, complete with videos, toilets, and perhaps a little kitchen. I don't like them personally as I always get a bit of travel sickness – and, of course, you can get hold-ups and traffic problems which cause delays.

Now and again we will go by plane, to far-off places like Portsmouth, or we'll fly back from London if we've had an evening game and it's too late for a train. The planes will be hired specially, just for the team, but they are small and seem to shake a lot, which I find scary.

I much prefer the train, and I think most of the lads do. Luckily, we used the train more and more as our normal transport last season. The club will book a whole first-class coach so we have privacy and can walk about, which is a bit of a plus. A train is also much better, of course, when it comes to playing cards.

If we're playing in London, the team coach will go ahead by road, and picks us up off the train at Euston and takes us to our hotel. Most of the time I don't know which hotel we're in. I can never remember the names or addresses. You just get so used to hotel life it all begins to feel the same.

You take for granted everything being done for you –

the travel arrangements, hotels and meals. It can make you spoiled for the real world, I suppose; but, on the other hand, the club's objective is to take away all possible aggravations. Even though I'm only 20, it's been like this practically all my life, at least since I was 13 and went to Switzerland for the youth tournament. All that's happened is that the hotels have got better.

Before a game, I don't really follow any set routine. And I don't have any superstitions, at least none that I'm aware of. Some players always walk out onto the pitch in the same order, such as last or second-last, and try to do so for every game if they think it will bring them luck. I'm told I usually seem to walk out after Rio and John O'Shea, or sometimes between them, but I don't do so deliberately. I just walk out with the lads I've been talking to as we've left the dressing room.

But I have noticed recently that I've acquired a habit I hadn't realised I had. Gary Neville pointed it out to me. Before we go out to warm up, I seem to go through my own little ritual. While I'm still sitting on my seat in the dressing room, under my number 8 shirt hanging up, I will put on my warm-up top, my slip and my shorts. Then, for some reason, I move somewhere else, such as the physio's room, to put on my socks and boots.

The physio had in fact noticed it as well as Gary. As far as I'm aware, there was no reason for it and I didn't see it as a good luck thing. I'll probably carry on doing it – or not. It doesn't bother me either way.

Rio has a pretty funny habit, but then he has lots of funny habits. As we leave the dressing room, and wait in the tunnel, whether for Man Utd or England, he pours a bottle of water over his head. He says it's to refresh himself. I think it's to make his hair grow. Then, as we get out on to the pitch, he jumps up and down on the spot, trying to make himself grow.

During a game I never hold back from arguing or shouting at anyone, if I think they're at fault. Roy Keane used to be the main shouter, but I wasn't scared of him. I'm not scared of anyone. What Roy was doing was trying to make you do the right things, whom to pass to and telling you where to be on the pitch. I didn't mind that. If you didn't listen to him, or just gave him a mouthful back, he'd give up on you in the end. His attitude was that it's your loss. Which was true.

I'll shout at anyone, even Gary Neville, if I have to.

In one match last season, I shouted and screamed at Patrice Evra to get into position when we were defending a corner. I'm noisier on the pitch than I am in real life simply because I want to win so much.

I probably shouted too much at referees in my early years. When I see video clips of that now, I realise I was sometimes over the top. It didn't do me any good and was a bit stupid because the refs are not going to change their minds. Today I still talk back at them, but I do it more calmly, and don't eff and blind at them. All the same, I think refs do get carried away by their own self-importance and tend to forget they are just refs, not superstars or TV personalities.

At Man Utd Coleen has bought an executive box so she can invite her family and friends to the game. After a home game, some of the players will go the players' lounge where their family and friends gather. I tend not to go, unless I'm meeting someone there. When we play away, we never visit our opponents' players' lounge. It's not being unsociable or superior, just that we all want to get in the coach and get home as soon as possible.

In the evening, if we've played at home, me and Coleen will usually go for a meal or a drink, sometimes with her parents.

Later, I always find it hard to sleep after any game. I keep on reliving what happened and what I should have done. I suppose it's the adrenaline still flowing. If we've lost or I've made some mistakes, I won't get to sleep until about three in the morning, just going over everything. I'll still be gutted. Even if we've won I still won't sleep. I'll be more relaxed and happy, but I'll still be reliving the whole game.

When I was younger, I got to sleep a lot more quickly. I don't know why, because I don't really feel more pressure today, even though the games are more important, hard, and exciting.

I still love playing as much as ever, can't wait for the kick-off, so it is a bit annoying not being able to sleep.

I suppose that's why I often fall asleep on the couch during the day.

I know a lot of players have said that they got more pleasure out of playing football at 15 years of age than at 25, the so-called height of their career. That's because of all the pressures, from the managers and coaches, the fans who expect so much, and the press always ready to hammer you. I honestly feel the opposite. I enjoy it more now than I did when I was younger – because now it's more competitive and hard, and a better standard. I also enjoy having 76,000 fans at Old Trafford shouting my name.

They've got a new song now. I couldn't actually understand the words at first, until someone told me. It's a sort of rap:

> 'I saw my friend the other day
> Who said he'd seen the white Pel-ay
> Wayne Roo-nay, Wayne Roo-nay
> He goes by the name of
> Wayne Roo-nay'

It's clean, too, which you can't say about all football chants, even those from your own supporters.

But the best moment in football for me is still the same – running out onto the pitch at three o'clock.

EIGHTEEN

Gambling

After Euro 2004 in Portugal, I had to put up with acres of press coverage about the fact that I had visited a massage parlour many years earlier. Just a few months before the World Cup of 2006 in Germany, I found myself again attracting lots of space and attention, keeping in business the clever columnists who were able to give us the benefit of their wise comments and inside knowledge. A joke.

This time the subject was gambling. As I've said earlier, my school report from De La Salle, when I was aged 14, had said I was distracted by gambling – although that was, in fact, only a game called Jingles in the school playground, when you'd win or lose £1 at most.

My dad has always liked a bet, putting a few pence each week on the horses, but obviously that's all he's ever had to spend, the odd bob – whatever a bob is. It's like 'turning on a tanner'; I've heard the older coaches use that phrase, again without knowing what it meant. Another ancient one is a 'thrupenny header', so-called when you head the ball and it goes in the opposite direction to the one you intended; apparently this refers to the very old three penny piece which had jagged edges.

I didn't do any proper gambling until about my second year at Everton when, by then, I was earning fairly good money. We were living in our house in Formby, where we were never quite happy, and on the way home from training, if I knew Coleen was not going to be there, I would stop at the bookies and put a few quid on a horse.

When I was sat at home on my own, watching horse racing, dog racing or a football match that I had no involvement with on TV, I'd often put on a bet just to make it more interesting. I wasn't putting on huge amounts, just a few hundreds at a time or perhaps a thousand now and again.

After about a year, though, I had lost about £50,000, which was stupid. When Coleen found out she was furious, and told me how daft I had been. I said I would give it up, which I did. For about a year I didn't put on a single bet.

Betting at a bookmaker's is always a bit public. Even if you ring one of the numbers you see advertised on TV, there's always the chance that your name and details will come out, that someone could leak the story to the press.

So that was always a slight worry, and actually helped me to stop betting for a long while.

When we travel with Manchester Utd, by coach or train, most people play cards, as they did at Everton. I always play the same game with the same people – Rio Ferdinand, Wes Brown, Darren Fletcher and John O'Shea. It's a game called Shit Head, a bit like poker but simpler, where a player puts down three cards at a time.

We don't play for money, as it's not allowed. I gather that, according to Bryan Robson, in the old days at United, the team did play for money, although only small amounts.

Today, it's just a fun thing with daft rules. If a player loses two games on the trot they are barred from speaking. They have to carry on playing in silence – which, of course, is hard for me as I rabbit on all the time. If they lose three games in a row then the others are allowed to flick their ears. It isn't painful, just embarrassing.

One day, someone in the England dressing room gave me the phone number of a private bookmaker who would always keep things confidential. The press claimed the player was Michael Owen. I honestly can't recall who it was, but it most definitely wasn't Michael, although I did know he used the same guy. So, around the beginning of September last season, I started putting on bets again.

The reasons for doing it were the same as before.

Gambling

Basically I did it out of boredom, while I was sitting around at home after training usually with Coleen out and the television on. I found myself putting on the odd bet, as it made watching sport on TV more interesting.

I placed all my bets by text. I never spoke to, or met, the bloke to whom I was sending my bets. I just knew him as Mike. At first, I'd just put on £100, but then it started creeping up into the thousands.

In the first few months I did well. On three separate occasions I won good sums which came to £51,000 in total. I was paid my winnings in cash, not by cheque, by a young lad who visited the training ground. I never received any receipts or anything.

Each time I gave the money to Coleen, who probably ended up buying stuff for the house. She'll batter me for saying that but I honestly can't remember anything more specific. However, she did tell me I was being stupid, and should stop before I started losing.

I carried on all over the winter, still betting by text. I knew by now that I was losing, but nothing was ever said and no balance or accounts were sent to me. So I never really knew how much I was down. But I had an idea I was doing badly and so did what most gamblers do: I chased my bets and tried to recoup my losses by putting on even bigger sums.

One night in February 2006, before we were about to play at Blackburn, I was in the team hotel when, at about eight o'clock, I received a text message from Mike saying I would have to do something about my balance, but, in the meantime, could I pay back the £51,000 I'd totted up so far?

I rang Paul, my agent, to confess to him what I'd done. He hadn't known until then that I'd started gambling again. I don't think it affected my game against Blackburn. It didn't dwell on my mind, although we did lose the game 4–3.

Paul contacted the bookie to discuss the situation. He told me it was bad and they were looking to recoup a lot of money. I knew I had run up debts, but I hadn't realised how serious it was. Despite what I earn I don't have lots of money lying around in cash – it was all tied up and invested for me, or put away in special accounts.

Paul then did some research. He tried to find out who this Mike character was, and asked to see his book-maker's licence. He discovered that, at the time of my betting with him, he didn't have a licence but was acting for someone who claimed they did.

Paul was furious – both with me and the bloke who'd been taking the bets. He thought it wasn't businesslike never to give me any accounts or keep me updated on what was happening, just let me go on and on without any warnings. Paul felt I had been taken advantage of, given that I was young and known to have a high income.

But I blame myself not the bookmaker. It was me who put on the bets. No-one forced me. Paul told me that under the laws of the land I wouldn't have to pay up as gambling debts are considered debts of honour and not enforceable by law.

Of course, eventually the story appeared in the papers. For those two months, after I'd first heard about it in the February, we kept it quiet while Paul was investigating. Then suddenly it came out. I don't know who told the press – certainly Paul wouldn't have done so.

But in a way I'm glad it did all come out. It shocked me into realising how much I'd been betting, and losing, and made me aware of just how stupid I had been.

I was surprised by all the attention it attracted. I hadn't been doing anything illegal after all. The whole country is mad about betting, and all the online poker and betting firms appear to be making fortunes. There are adverts everywhere – on TV, in newspapers and on hoardings at football grounds – encouraging people to put on a bet; they make it so quick and easy. I was watching a match on Sky the other day, and right up to the last five minutes of the game the bookies were quoting odds on what the final score might be.

I suppose what created all the attention was the alleged large sums I'd lost, and the scale of my gambling. Some papers tried to suggest it would affect my play, that I'd be worrying about my gambling debts, but that was rubbish. I scored two goals in the next game against Spurs after the news broke in the newspapers.

It never would have affected me anyway. I saw it purely as a bit of fun to pass the time. I was happy when

I won and gutted when I lost. But that was it. I'd switch off the TV and forget it. It didn't dwell on my mind.

What did anger me was all the ex-players coming out and being so pious, telling me what a bad lad I'd been, how I'd gone wrong, and that I should not have been tempted. Yet they must surely understand; they know what happens in the dressing room, what some lads do when they suddenly have a lot of money at a very young age, and how they get through all those boring afternoons when they are supposed to be resting. It's always happened in football – it's just today the wages are so much bigger.

Paul Merson is supposed to have lost several millions of pounds during his football career. I don't know whether that's true or not, but it makes me realise that I could have got myself into a far worse mess.

The papers also tried to suggest that I'd fallen out with Michael Owen, that I was blaming it all on him. That's total rubbish. The press said that to make their stories seem more important, and to suggest how it could affect England's chances if there was tension between us. I've never discussed my betting with Michael, before or afterwards – I did everything at home on my own – and we're still the same good friends we have always been.

Anyway, it was quickly settled. I won't be betting with them anymore, and don't intend to ever get into that sort of mess again.

Gambling

Will I bet again? I may now and again, but in the normal way, settling up as I go along. I won £5,000 by backing the winner of the Cheltenham Gold Cup. That was good. But I'll only bet occasionally, when it's a big event. I've promised Paul and Coleen that I'll keep it well under control in future.

The Boss did have a private word with me when the story came out. But it wasn't really a bollocking. He agreed players have always liked a bet, but said to keep it in moderation, or I could lose all my money.

On top of that, in April 2006, I was involved in a legal case which had been going on for a long time. A year earlier, *The Sun* had alleged that I had slapped Coleen in a club in Cheshire. They used headlines like 'Crazed Rooney Thumps Coleen' and 'You Brute'. The *News of the World* then piled in, saying I had been guilty of a 'violent and nasty assault' on her. It was said I had slapped her across the face, punched her in the ribs and then told her to 'F*** off home'.

It was all rubbish – I had not touched her in any way. But the allegation was so serious that we agreed to consult solicitors to clear my name. Ian Monk, the publicist and PR for me and Coleen recommended the firm Schillings to Paul. The case was due to go to the High Court in April 2006 but was settled on the courtroom steps. News International admitted the story was totally false and had to print an apology.

What actually happened was this: one evening, in April 2005, a group of us from Manchester Utd had met up at Rio Ferdinand's house. Apart from me and Rio, there was Wes Brown, John O'Shea and Roy Carroll, plus our respective girlfriends. The girls were all chatting together while we were watching Real Madrid on the TV, and the plan was that we'd all later go out to have a meal.

But when the game finished, the lads suddenly decided to go off to a pub – on our own. I'm not saying whose idea it was, but, yeah, it was a bit sneaky. So we slipped off to have something to eat and left the girls behind. They were not exactly chuffed.

Later on, we all met up at a club at Alderley Edge. When the girls arrived some were naturally still hacked off that we had nicked off without them. Coleen and I did have a bit of an argument, I admit that, but that's all it was – just a few words. She wasn't happy I'd gone off with the lads and told me so. And that was it. All over.

Coleen had to get up early the next morning to fly to Cyprus for a photoshoot, so had to leave the club before the others. But she didn't leave alone – I went with her. We'd long finished arguing by then and went home happily together.

I presume someone must have heard us arguing, then saw us leaving early, and just made up the rest of it. They got it all wrong. I never touched Coleen, never have and never would. So when the story came out I was furious and, of course, so was Coleen. In fact, she was devastated.

We were awarded damages of around £100,000, plus all costs, and I gave it all away to three charities. Some went to Alderhey Children's Hospital in Liverpool, some to SOS Children's Charity, and some to Claire House. Rosie, Coleen's sister who is ill with Rhetts Syndrome, goes to Claire House every now and then, and one weekend every other month. It's a kind of rest home for sick kids, and is a brilliant place which does so much good. I have taken part in various charity events for them over the last few years.

Around the same time, there was a third issue in the papers that was upsetting. The *Daily Mail* had maintained that, at Coleen's 20th birthday party in April 2006, our two families, the Rooneys and the McLoughlins, had to be kept apart in separate rooms in case they all started fighting.

The paper had referred back to the party where supposedly our two families had got embroiled in a punch-up and the police had to be called – which, as I've already said, wasn't true and was simply some of my family arguing with the bouncers.

On this latest occasion, there was actual proof, which we could show quickly, that the story was untrue – because my family was not even at the party. It's not often that things are so simple to put right and when this was pointed out the paper did at least have the decency to print an immediate correction.

You may wonder why we bothered. Why not just ignore what the *Daily Mail* said? Yet there are some stories that are so serious, hurtful and damaging, such as me supposedly having slapped Coleen, that they can't be ignored.

When it's just about me, such as the gambling story, then I have to take it and can't really protest. But when it affects your family or your fiancée, and the awful things that get written then get repeated in the papers forever, you have to try and stop them, or at least get them corrected if you can. That is why we have a publicist. We need to monitor dialogue with the papers and we need someone who can speak to them when stories are wrong or misrepresented.

At the age of only 20, I seem to have stacked up acres of newspaper space about things me and Coleen have done, or are supposed to have done. I certainly never expected any of that when I joined Everton's School of Excellence at the age of nine.

I'm sure I've kept a good many lawyers off the streets, and provided them with loads of work and stacks of fees – something else I'd never thought I would be doing when I was just a kid back in Croxteth. In that way, I have definitely helped the economy. Not just the book-makers.

NINETEEN

My First Trophy

Manchester United finished third in the FA Premiership in my first season with them, and we didn't get beyond the last sixteen in the European Champions League. We were beaten in the FA Cup Final and in the semis of the Carling Cup. So you couldn't exactly say it had been a brilliant season, not by United's standards. No medals and no pots. How my old Everton mates loved it: 'Thought you'd joined The Scum to win something? Ha ha ha.'

So we were all determined that the 2005/06 season would be a lot better, with something to show for it at the end. There were no big signings, money-wise, but Edwin van der Sar, the Dutch player, came from Fulham as our new goalie and South Korea's Park Ji-sung arrived from PSV Eindhoven in Holland – both looked like good buys – while Phil Neville and Roy Carroll left for Everton and West Ham respectively. We all hoped Ole Gunnar Solskjaer would soon be back from injury and skipper Roy Keane would stay fit.

August started off well, and I scored in each of my first three games – for United in the first round of the European Champions League against Debreceni which we won 3–0; in the Premiership against, guess who, Everton (2–0); and for England in a friendly against Denmark (4–1).

Things didn't go quite so well afterwards, though, especially in Europe. We just couldn't hardly seem to score, stuttering to a 0–0 draw away against Villarreal and later being beaten 1–0 in Lille and 2–1 at Benfica.

I was sent off in Spain against Villarreal. I'd received a yellow card after a tackle. I thought their fella had dived and conned the ref, so I decided to applaud the decision which, of course, was stupid – and the yellow was turned into a red.

We were out of Europe by Christmas and hadn't even made it out of the group stage, which was worse than the year before. A disaster.

In the second half of the season we fared much better, although there was no real reason for it. In the first half of the campaign, we had lost Roy Keane to Celtic. Roy was a huge miss, both as a player and a character in the dressing room. Then Paul Scholes suffered an eye injury and was set to be out for months. He's our playmaker and gets us passing the ball, so that was more bad news.

Other players got injured as well, but they came back more quickly. Giggsy and John O'Shea had taken over the midfield from Keane and Scholes and, as the season developed, they formed a good partnership. Being knocked out of Europe, and out of the FA Cup by February, when Liverpool beat us 1–0, meant we didn't have too many other distractions. We could concentrate on doing well in the League and in the Carling Cup.

We reached the final of the Carling Cup to play Wigan at the Millennium Stadium in Cardiff. With all due respect to Wigan, who had just come up from the Championship and were having an excellent season, we were expected to beat them. It would have been absolutely awful if we hadn't, and the prospect always makes it a bit worrying as these things can happen. But, on the day, we played very well. Me and Ronny were probably the men of the match and I bagged two goals as we won 4–0. The first came from a flicked header by Louis Saha which the defenders failed to deal with and I slotted it in, and the other followed a free-kick which Rio headed on to me.

It was my first ever trophy and my first ever medal professionally. The club didn't organise any special celebrations or events for afterwards, though, as it was still the middle of the League season and we were desperate to close the gap to Chelsea who, by now, were miles in front. At one stage they had been 18 points ahead of us.

After arriving back in Manchester following the Carling Cup Final, me, Coleen and her two younger brothers went out for a Chinese meal at a restaurant called Wings. Yeah, not exactly a huge celebration, but my thinking was that after the World Cup will be the time to have a really big celebration party . . .

Towards the end of the season we hit a good run, winning most of our games, and got to within seven points of Chelsea who appeared to be faltering slightly. For months most people had thought the destiny of the title was a foregone conclusion and Chelsea would walk it. But now there was a chink, a slight hope we might even overhaul them right at the end of the season.

On 14 April, we had to entertain Sunderland who were already relegated, so obviously we fancied it. A win would have been our tenth on the trot and would have brought us to within four points of Chelsea.

We were rubbish though. The game ended 0–0 and their goalie, Kelvin Davis, was brilliant; in fact, they could have won as they had some good chances.

In the dressing room afterwards I'd never seen The Boss so angry. He knew we had now ruined whatever small chance we still had of winning the League. He said the whole team had played badly – but then, in front of everyone, singled out me and Ronny for particular blame, telling us we had both been 'f***ing shite'. Then he just walked out, furious.

Afterwards, talking to the press, he didn't swear but he also didn't mince his words: 'Rooney and Ronaldo are both kids and they've got to learn, but we can wait for two or three years to get the full benefit of them.

This photo was taken by Jason Bell, who flew in from New York just to snap me! I thought he did a great job and so did my sponsors Coca-Cola – more importantly Coleen likes it too.

ABOVE: Another award – the 2005 FIFPro World Player XI. I see my tie is undone again! I hate wearing ties anyway.

BELOW: I much prefer a T-shirt, and a good laugh.

The Carling Cup Final 2006 against Wigan, my first of two goals...

...which pleased the Man Utd fans, especially this lad who I first met the day I signed...

THANK YOU FOR ROONEY!

...and I was also pleased when we won 4–0, my first major professional trophy. Here I am with the Man of the Match award.

LEFT: Official ambassador for SOS Children's Charity. I like to give something back, especially to kids less fortunate than me.

RIGHT: A good night for me is staying in with the telly, but Coleen does enjoy taking her handbags out. Note the bow-tie. Don't say I don't make an effort sometimes.

BELOW: The house on the right was the first home I bought my Mum and Dad when I signed my professional contract with Everton.

ABOVE: 29 April 2006, at Stamford Bridge against Chelsea, a day I won't forget, the day my metatarsal went, the day I thought my World Cup dreams were over...

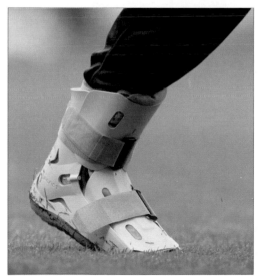

ABOVE: It was worse than I'd feared – I'd fractured the fourth metatarsal in my right foot and also chipped the third metatarsal. I'd be six weeks out, at least, before I could even train.

RIGHT: The Boss, Sir Alex, warned me not to set my heart on playing in the World Cup, so that if I did, it would be a bonus.

LEFT: In five weeks, I was training with England again as they prepared for two friendlies at Old Trafford.

RIGHT: A moment I never thought would happen. Coming on for England against Trinidad & Tobago in our second group game in World Cup 2006.

FAR RIGHT: David Beckham had just scored from a brilliant free-kick against Ecuador. Before the game I'd joked with him: 'You'll score today because you've been s**t in training all week!'

RIGHT: Prince William, President of the FA and a footie fan, came to check on my progress, which was kind.

BELOW: Showing passion for the fans and playing for England. I did this for my sponsors Nike ahead of the World Cup.

Against Sweden we drew 2–2 and I was on from the beginning for the first time…

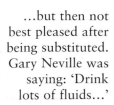

…but then not best pleased after being substituted. Gary Neville was saying: 'Drink lots of fluids…'

LEFT: The quarter-final in Gelsenkirchen. Me as the lone striker, surrounded by five Portuguese defenders.

It was an accident. I was off-balance and my foot landed awkwardly…

…but to my amazement, the ref took out the red.

We lost on penalties. Again. I watched from the dressing room.

Tonight, they probably had their worst performances of the season, but we know they will be great players.

'All the hype that is placed on Wayne has borne fruit tonight. People have to remember he's only a kid. Saying he's going to be responsible for winning England the World Cup is the biggest nonsense I've heard in my life.'

What he said was true, we were rubbish. But I don't think it was because of any World Cup pressure I might have been under. It was just one of those nights. We were shite and I was shite. So The Boss was right again.

England, meanwhile, still had to get through their World Cup qualifying group. We had a win against Wales on 3 September, then, four days later, we travelled to Belfast to meet Northern Ireland whom we were expected to thump.

From the beginning it all went wrong. Sven had decided on a 4–5–1 formation, which could adapt if necessary to 4–3–3, with Michael Owen on his own up front, and me and Shaun Wright-Phillips on the wings. We'd practised it in training all week, and were all happy with it. But the minute we kicked off we could tell it wasn't working and, playing out wide, I just wasn't getting the ball.

It was the worst England game I'd played in – and the worst for me personally. I was devastated. I caught one of their players with my elbow, which was not deliberate, but simply due to getting worked up and trying too hard to get the ball.

It was during that game that Becks put his arm round me on the touchline while I was het up, and the fans watching on TV clearly saw me tell him to 'F*** off.'

I earned some stick from the press for that, especially as Becks was the England captain, but it was meaningless really. David understood. Like most players, I spend a lot of time during every game, and in training, shouting at the other players, ticking them off and telling them what they should have done or should be doing. So I wasn't ashamed of saying what I did to Becks, and neither did I regret it. It's what happens in the heat of a game.

But I was ashamed of the result. Being beaten 1–0 by Northern Ireland was utter humiliation. They deserved the win on the day, but we were awful. I hope never to have to go through that again.

However, after that we never played anywhere near as badly again. Poland were thought to be our closest rivals but we beat them 2–1 in October 2005 to win the group. In November we saw off Argentina 3–2 in a friendly, with me scoring once, and the following March we defeated Uruguay 2–1. In the end, we had qualified for the 2006 World Cup finals fairly easily.

Early in April 2006, for the second season running, I was elected as the PFA Young Player of the Year. I had also beaten my previous year's tally, with 19 goals, the biggest number in one season in my career to date.

As the season was drawing to a close, I was thinking that I'd done pretty well. And while United may have done badly in Europe and the FA Cup, we were giving Chelsea a run for their money by beginning to close the gap and ensuring that they wouldn't run away with the league long before the season had ended.

So, personally, following what I felt had been a decent season for me, I was ready and eager for the World Cup finals ahead.

For a start, I felt better physically. At Everton I'd often felt knackered, and even in my first season at Manchester Utd I may have tried a bit too hard, both in training and on the pitch.

This last season, though I'd felt good in training all the time. I became used to United's methods, and in games I didn't lose my temper in silly ways – well, not as often as I'd done in the past anyway.

Perhaps it's all to do with age. At 20, I am beginning to get more mature – at long last some people might say. I am also more experienced as a player with four premier league seasons behind me. But I know I have a long way to go. I must keep improving and learning; my heading and my left foot could both be better.

I don't think my improvement during 2005/06 was anything to do with how I'd been playing in the team or its line-up. It might have looked, from the outside, with Roy Keane gone and Paul Scholes out, that I had been taking more control in midfield, dominating more, starting more attacks, spreading the ball around more, and laying on goal scoring passes instead of always trying to score myself.

It is true that I like laying on a goal, and I attempt to do that more now than when I was 13 or 14, when I simply went head down for goal. But my position or part in the team, either for Manchester Utd or England, has changed. I still see myself as a striker, not a midfield player, and prefer to play just behind the main frontman, as I'd been doing all season. And I've always gone back to defend – I see that as part of my job.

The previous season at United, I was played more wide, in a 4–5–1 or 4–3–3 formation, and Sven had also tried that for England, with me again out wide. Personally I prefer a traditional 4–4–2, though, and played that all this last season for both Manchester Utd and England – which, in truth, is probably why I played so well and was so happy.

So, naturally, as we approached the end og the season, I was hoping and praying that my form would continue into the World Cup. All the papers were saying I was the vital man which was nice, but I tend to take their comments with a pinch of salt. And the established England stars, like Stevie, John Terry and Frank Lampard, all said during interviews that I was their big hope. Everyone was saying that England had their best squad, and their best chance, for years.

My First Trophy

I didn't see it as an added pressure. I'm fortunate in playing as the second striker for England and Man United; the main striker, such as Michael Owen, or Ruud, has much more pressure. If they don't score for a run of games everyone gets on at them. Scoring is what they are expected to do. So, if they are not it's very hard for them.

With me, I like to think I offer something different to just scoring goals. I don't *have* to score, yet, even if I don't, I can still be considered to have had a good game. That's a big advantage, and helps take the heat off any pressure I might otherwise feel. But, honestly, these sort of expectations aren't a burden. Perhaps it's my age, or my lack of World Cup experience, but, ahead of the tournament, I didn't feel at all nervous, only excited. I love the big stage.

Then came *that* game against Chelsea, almost at the end of the season, at Stamford Bridge on 29 April 2006.

The previous season, at Old Trafford, when Chelsea had already won the Premiership title, The Boss made us stand out on the pitch and clap them when they came on. A nice, gentlemanly gesture, I suppose, but I hated doing it, and I think most of our players and fans felt the same. Perhaps that was a bit of psychology by The Boss. I wanted to be the winner, not having to clap someone else for winning. And especially not at our place, in front of our home crowd.

If Chelsea had beaten us that day, they would have won the League there and then, so we were keen to do well. We were coming in on a good run, having got 31 points out of a possible 33.

The night before, in our hotel, The Boss banned any outsiders from coming into the hotel to see us, even family and friends. He wanted total concentration.

We obviously hadn't been doing much concentration in the fourth minute when William Gallas scored their first goal. And there was worse to come. From all points of view.

That was the game when I thought the end of the world had come.

TWENTY

Me and My Metatarsal

It was in the Whalley Range Hospital, back in Manchester after the Chelsea game, that it was officially confirmed my metatarsal had gone.

Around ten o'clock, Coleen's Uncle Sean came to pick me up in his car. He took me to his house where I had a meal. Coleen had nipped to a girlfriend's birthday party. I waited until she had finished, then I joined her at her parents' house where we spent the next three nights. The club said I had to rest for two whole days at home.

They fitted me with an air boot to protect my foot and I also had crutches, so I did nothing much in those two days, just sat around, resting, watching TV. Much like normal, I suppose, except this time I'd done no training and didn't know what was going to happen, or when.

They were saying it would be about six weeks, at least, before I could even start football training. I kept thinking about how it had taken me 96 days after the last metatarsal injury before I could play, but of course there were differences. It was at the time I was being transferred from Everton to Man Utd, so for one reason or other, Everton were not in quite such a panic to get me fit. I suppose they didn't want me injured again before they'd got their money. And then when I got to Man Utd, The Boss wanted me absolutely fit and in tip-top condition for my debut, and not to risk anything.

I also began to learn there was a difference in the injury. Last time it had been my fifth metatarsal, which is part of the very little toe – it's right on the edge of your foot, with no protection. So it's easy to make it worse, if you lean too hard or put too much pressure on that side. With the fourth metatarsal, the bone is more protected, on either side. In theory, it should heal quicker, if you are sensible and do all the right things. So that cheered me up a bit. It was also on the base of my foot so that was also better.

After three days, I went to United's training ground and started fitness treatment. During that first week, I spent two hours in the gym every day, on the treadmill and also doing some light weights, just to keep my strength and fitness up, making sure I didn't put on weight. I also went swimming in the club's pool.

I didn't enjoy that gym work. I wanted to be outside on the training pitch, with a ball. In my whole football career, I'd never done as much gym work as this, on weights and stuff. With my physique I don't normally need to.

The Boss gave me a talk about not setting my heart on playing in the World Cup. That way, if I wasn't ready in time, I wouldn't be disappointed. But then if I did make it, which he hoped I would, it would be a huge bonus.

I went to watch United's last two games, on my crutches – and I hated it, every minute. I sat up in the stand, where of course I'd never sat before since I'd made my debut. It was terrible, watching the team play, watching movements develop, yet not being part of it. I was kicking every ball in my mind. It was agony.

Luckily, it was the end of the season, not the beginning. If it had been the start, I would have stopped going. I think it's better when you're injured not to watch football at all. It's too unbearable.

At home, at the end of the first week, I was taking my boot off in the house, which I wasn't supposed to do, walking around for a bit in my bare foot. The pain seemed much less.

The papers were full of the story, all about me being irreplaceable, the country's talisman, and how England now wouldn't win the World Cup. It was flattering, I suppose, but rubbish. I knew it wouldn't upset the lads, nor make them either jealous or angry. They all know as well as I do how the press behave – they have to put a spin on their stories. It's not enough to simply report my injury – they have to take it further, make it not just bad news for me, but for the team, for the nation. All the lads understand that. They've been through it.

I know England are not a one-man band, so do they. We have many vital players we can't afford to lose – Becks, Owen, Stevie, Lampard and others. Without me, they could still win. I know that, and they know that, so no, I wasn't bothered by all the stories. I spoke to several of the players on the phone, the likes of Becks and Stevie, just telling them how I was, with them wishing me luck.

After the FA Cup Final, in which Stevie was brilliant, the press rather changed their story a bit – they were now saying that Stevie could replace me, and play further forward, score more goals in my place, so all was not lost. They were getting hopeful again. And it's true. Stevie is brilliant. He can play in any position, depending on where Sven wants to put him.

Then there was a new big football story – Sven had surprised everyone by picking Theo Walcott in the squad, without ever seeing him play, and without him ever playing in the Premiership. I admit I was surprised. I had seen Theo a couple of times on TV when he'd been with Southampton, but that was all. But he must have been doing something right at Arsenal, to make Arsène Wenger so confident about him.

I was pleased for him, and for the team. It didn't put any extra pressure on me, that he might take my place.

He's a different sort of player. I never feel any pressure anyway. I know that the fans who watch me know I will always give 100 percent, that I will always try my hardest.

The arrival of Walcott on the scene at only seventeen didn't suddenly make me feel old, though I suppose I am, by comparison, with my 29 caps. And his arrival didn't make me think back to my debut for England when I was his age.

I suppose what I did feel was sorry for him. I saw him being built up so much by the press and I knew what was to come. Because there's bound to be a backlash. Having built him up, they'll then have to knock him down, either because of his performances or something off the pitch. While he doesn't play, he'll be okay. They'll all love him. Then when he does, in due course they'll have a go at him. That's how things work.

It's not for me to give him any advice. I suppose if he ever asked me, I would say he should listen to his manager and don't get involved in too much stuff off the pitch. He has to pick and choose what commercial and media stuff he does, and he shouldn't do too much of it at first, not for a while anyway. But it's up to him. He'll make his own decisions. He'll learn as he goes along, as I did.

In my second full week of recuperation from my injury, I was put into an oxygen tank. This was a huge thing, a mobile one, which the club had hired. It was parked at the ground so I could use it every day. By going inside it, and breathing in all that oxygen, it's supposed to help the healing process. That's roughly the theory, I think.

I had to do it for 100 minutes twice a day, with a five-hour break between each session. So I set my alarm for 6.15 in the morning and got to the training ground by seven. I wanted to get my first session in as quickly as possible. During the five hours in between the sessions, I went to the gym, did my fitness work, then just hung around and waited for the next session.

After that first day, and the two sessions, I felt sick. And I hated being in the tank. I told the doctor and he said that happens sometimes. It would get better. I just had to persevere and get in more sessions.

I couldn't drive, of course, for those first two weeks, as my foot was still in the special air boot and I was meant to put no pressure on it. So Kona, from Proactive, my management company, drove me to and from training every day.

It was funny hearing him talking about the World Cup – because he was definitely going and I wasn't definitely going. His brother, Shaka Hislop, Trinidad and Tobago's goalie, like all players in the World Cup, gets two free tickets, plus another eight which have to be bought. Kona and his girlfriend were going on Shaka's two tickets. It's a huge thing for them, coming from such a small country, getting to the World Cup for the first time. Dwight Yorke, the team captain and former United striker, was training at our place at the end of the season, so I talked to him quite a bit.

Kona gets a lot of stick at work because we have one or two Irish blokes who are furious their country is not going. He had to book his holidays in advance, to get time off to go and watch Trinidad and Tobago in Germany. On the journeys back and forth, he was always telling me that he might need more time off – if Trinidad stuff England and get to the final. No chance, of course.

I did eight sessions in all in that oxygen tank, and it never got any better. I felt sick all the time. I hated being stuck inside for so long, just lying there as if I was dead, listening to the hum of the machine. After four days, it had made me feel so weak I wasn't up to doing all my training. That's when they decided to pack it in.

I don't know whether or not it did any good. It certainly didn't feel like it to me. According to the medical staff, they don't know either. It seems to work for some, but not for others.

In the third week, at long last, I was allowed out of the gym and could ride around outside on a mountain bike. That was a great relief, just being in the fresh air.

One of the people who kept me going was Alan Smith. During all this time, the training ground was almost empty. It was the close season, everyone away or on holiday, except for any long-term injured players, such as Alan.

Smudge, as he's called at the club, suffered a most horrific injury several months previously. It was during the away game against Liverpool. I remember it very well. He went into a tackle very hard with John Arne Riise to block the ball, and went down like a bag of sand. I didn't realise how serious it was, or what really had happened. I went across and took hold of his head. 'Come on, get up,' I said to him. Then I suddenly noticed his face. He wasn't just in agony. His face had gone white. I'd never seen such a thing before.

Then I looked down at his foot. God, it was horrible. Even though he still had his boot and sock on, I could see that his ankle had come out of its socket. His foot was sticking sideways, at the weirdest angle. I felt sick in my stomach.

Poor Smudge had not just broken his leg, but dislocated his ankle and damaged his ligaments. That's why he'd been out for such a long time.

But he was now progressing well. It was good to be out with him, on our mountain bikes, having a few laughs and jokes. As all players say, the thing you miss most when you're injured, apart from playing, is the dressing room, the banter and mucking around with the lads in the squad.

I then had another CT scan and it seemed to suggest I was progressing well, at least nothing had gone wrong, but they couldn't give me a date when I'd start full training.

I felt so good, and the pain had gone, that I began to get hopeful. At the beginning, we'd been reckoning on six weeks to get over the injury and be fit enough to start training. I was now beginning to think, well, I could be ready in five weeks, if I kept up the good progress.

I never got really depressed. I didn't sit around and mope or moan – no more than I normally do. Coleen and her family and my family were all supportive, saying I was going to make it. The evening I was told it was definitely a break, in fact two, was the worst. And then I didn't like all that gym work. It was a drag because there was so little variety. Apart from all that, though, I wasn't too fed up.

But once I started more varied training, on the mountain bike and stuff, I enjoyed it more, felt I was progressing and had things to aim for and work through. I told myself that if I tried my best, and did everything I was told, then I'd have a good chance.

If not, if a scan showed I still didn't have a cat in hell's chance, then we'd go off on holiday. That's what I told Coleen. We'd at least get something out of it. Go off on a luxury hols.

I had finished in the gym one day when I heard that Coleen's house had been vandalised. Her dad Tony loves his house and has worked so hard to make it nice. It was the council house in which he brought up his family, but then he bought it outright and added bits on. Coleen wanted him to move somewhere more private, now that she has money of her own, but he's always refused.

Three cars parked outside the house had their windows broken. One of them belonged to me and one was the people carrier which is used to take Rosie to her hospice.

I don't think it was connected with the fact that Coleen had just been on TV, being interviewed by Trevor McDonald, about the work of children's hospices. She was brilliant in the interview, very sincere. I was proud of her.

I also don't think the damage was aimed at me personally, just because I left Everton and went to Manchester Utd. It might have been part of it, but I doubt it. Of course, everyone around there knows whose house it is, knows about me and my relatives. But I honestly think it was just daft lads, coming home pissed or drugged up, who decided to do it for a laugh, without really thinking. It was disgusting, of course. And they did it in the dark. I think they'd have been too scared to do it during the daytime.

Coleen's mum and the rest of the family now want to move, to somewhere more private with a security gate, so that kind of thing can't happen again. Although Tony still doesn't want to, he will do what is best for his family. I respect him for that.

*   *   *

The highlight of the fourth week was The Party. Me and Coleen took a private jet, arranged by Paul and the Proactive office, from Manchester to Luton airport. It's now become too much of a hassle to go almost anywhere by train or even by road. Since the injury, there were even more reporters and photographers hanging around the training ground, trying to get pictures.

We then had a chauffeur drive us to David Beckham's house, the so-called Beckingham Palace. I'd been there before, but this time we weren't inside much as the party took place in a big marquee.

We were told to come 'Full Length and Fabulous' which I took to mean evening suits. I wore mine, but I didn't put on a bow tie. I hate bow ties. I can't wear them, I think my neck must be too big. But I did wear a plain black tie. Coleen was in, er, let me see, a green frock, yeah, I think it was green. She looked fabulous.

We sat on a table with four other couples. There was Gary Neville and his girl, Ashley Cole and his girlfriend, Cheryl Tweedy from Girls Aloud, Andrew Flintoff, the England cricketer, was with his, plus there was a friend of Becks from Manchester.

The meal was good. It began with soup, can't remember what sort, and then chicken. Gordon Ramsey did the cooking. I don't know anything about him or his restaurants, though I gather he's very famous. There was pudding, but I didn't have any. I enjoyed it.

There were lots of celebrities present, but I didn't recognise most of them. The only one I spoke to was Sharon Osbourne. She was with Ozzy. Our chat lasted about ten seconds. Someone told me later that David Cameron [Leader of the Conservative Party] was there, but I never saw him. I wouldn't have recognised him anyway.

There was a big auction afterwards, for charity of course. The rapper P. Diddy got up and said he was auctioning a weekend for two at his home in New York. I didn't know it was coming up, no-one had told me about it. Rio Ferdinand was at the table next to us and he leaned over and said to me, 'How about you and me bidding?' 'Yeah, go on,' I said. 'We'll go halves.'

We won it – with a bid of £150,000, shared between us. We were dead chuffed. We're both big fans of P. Diddy. So I'm hoping me and Rio can get over to P. Diddy's place sometime in the summer.

Afterwards, there was music and entertainment and dancing – and yes, I did have a dance. Nothing too energetic. I didn't do my Michael Jackson impersonation. That's the one Coleen doesn't like me doing. She says it's embarrassing. But I did get up and do a bit, despite my foot. I think having a few drinks always helps with any pain. Only joking.

We got back to our hotel at about four o'clock. I wasn't drunk, but I'd had quite a bit. I enjoyed it all. Meeting up with all the England lads was good, better than being stuck on my own in the gym.

The vital day for me was going to be Thursday, 25 May. That's when I was due to have my next CT scan, at the Whalley Range hospital, four weeks after the injury first occurred. The medical people had told me that if they could see callouses growing over the injury, that would be a good sign, showing that the bone was healing. I'd then be able to move on to the next stage – doing some jogging at last, then twisting and turning, then full training with the lads.

I had set my heart on joining the squad at the Lowry Hotel on the Sunday, three days later. I knew I wouldn't be able to train with them, but I'd feel part of the squad. I'd be able to go on the England coach every day to training at Carrington.

It was lucky for me that England's two pre-World Cup friendlies were both going to be played at Old Trafford, against Hungary and Jamaica. Nice and handy. I could carry on with my own fitness programme at the same place as they were training. I'd be with the squad, if not actually *in* the squad.

Obviously, I had no chance of playing in either of the friendlies, or even the first of the group games. I wasn't that optimistic. But I was reckoning, if all went well, and if the scan showed definite healing, I'd be ready to play in the third group game, against Sweden. Or at least I'd be on the bench.

The day before the scan, after attending the gym and some bike work, I had a little knockabout with the ball. Nothing strenuous. Just passing it back and forward over ten yards with one of the youth team players. No-one else was around. I know I shouldn't have done, but I couldn't help it. Just to touch a ball again. No pain or problem. It felt brilliant.

The result of the CT scan was inconclusive. But it wasn't bad. As so often happens, you build yourself up, waiting for a medical report, thinking it's going to settle things one way or the other. Either I'd definitely be playing very soon, or that would be it, might as well go off to Barbados.

If there had been definite calcification – I think that's the word, meaning it was regrowing – that would have been excellent and I could have got the all-clear to start proper training. No calcification would have been bad news, and I would have been out of it. They could see some calcification, but only at the bottom end. It showed the injury had not yet fully healed – but, on the other hand, it was progressing okay, after four weeks.

It was a bit disappointing really as I wasn't as far ahead as I'd led myself to believe. It was just normal. After all, they had said at the beginning it would be six weeks at least before I could think about training properly.

Some of the papers had been making out that The Boss didn't want me to go at all, to save me for Man

Utd, that he was rowing with Sven who had been giving the impression I'd definitely make it. In private, he had always been encouraging, giving me hope, saying he definitely wanted me to play in the World Cup. It would help my development as a player. He just wanted to play down the press speculation, keep things calm, and not put too much pressure on me.

He's been through this so many times. It took Becks eight weeks to get over his metatarsal injury while Gary Neville was out for over four months, because of complications. He told me that the fact I didn't feel any pain was meaningless, at my age. It didn't mean it had healed. I would just have to be patient and keep up the gym work.

However, it was agreed I could join up with the England squad. But I'd have to have another scan on 7 June. Only then would they know if I was fit enough to resume full football training.

So it was a bit of a sickener in a way, and not what I'd expected. I'd been told I now had no chance at all of starting the first couple of matches. The best I could hope for was to be available for either Sweden or the round-of-16 game . . .

TWENTY-ONE

The Scan

It was strange joining up with the England squad at the Lowry Hotel in Manchester. It was as if I hadn't seen them for a long time, yet all I had missed really was the five days of their warm up in Portugal. Coleen had been looking forward to that, to sunbathing on the beach, meeting and chatting all evening to the other girls, having a few drinks. I don't sunbathe, not with my pale skin. I always have to wear a T-shirt or some sort of covering over my shoulders, just in case. If I'm not careful, I go red and then I burn, even with the smallest amount of sun.

I gather most of the lads played golf in the afternoons, so I didn't really miss that either. I don't play golf, mainly because I'm no good at it and don't really know how, though on England get-togethers I usually go out on the golf course with them a few times, just to smash the ball.

On joining the England squad, I congratulated Steve McClaren, as it was the first time I'd seen him since he'd been made the new England manager-to-be. I asked him if he'd stop cheating, once he becomes the boss.

This is an old joke between us. In England training, I usually do a bit of two-touch passing with him – which means you pass the ball back and forward between the two of you, taking no more than two touches. Every time you make a mistake – can't control the ball, or take more than two touches – the other person gets a point. The first to ten is the winner.

When I play with Steve, he never seems to make a mistake. It's always your fault if he miscontrols it, your fault if he gets given a bad ball. Funny how it turns out that he wins every time. That's why I always call him a cheat.

But he's a good coach, always smiling. I'm glad he's got the job. I think he was the best Englishman available.

We've had our little moments over the years, me and Steve, as you always do with coaches. That's their job, to give you a bollocking now and again. He had a right go at me after that Northern Ireland humiliation in Belfast. He said I hadn't done my job right. My behaviour on the pitch hadn't been good. I agreed with him.

I felt a bit sad though that Sven was going. I think he was forced out by the press. They got him backed into a corner. I always found him a very clever man and a good manager. The press didn't seem to like him, but I don't know why. They said he wasn't emotional enough.

And it's true I never saw him lose his temper, or shout. But I think he was emotional, deep down. He just didn't show it in the normal way, but he did care. People show emotion in different ways. With him, it was inside his body. I always liked his style, his calm manner.

He did do his homework, prepared well, got his points across clearly. Best of all, he always trusted the players 100 per cent. I do like a manager who does that, who doesn't treat us like kids.

And I think he is good on tactics. I remember the friendly against Argentina back in November when he brought on Peter Crouch, which surprised a few people – but it meant their defenders were so busy watching him that Michael Owen managed to get two goals.

The press also said the reason we all liked him, the players I mean, was because he was soft and we could take advantage of him. It's true that you don't have to like a manager, it's not part of his job to be liked, but we liked Sven. Nobody took any liberties with him and neither would I call him soft.

I met Theo Walcott for the first time when I joined the lads at the Lowry, and also Aaron Lennon, though I had played against him at Spurs. Until their arrival in the England squad, I'd always been the youngest, ever since my first cap, three years earlier. It was good to see some young new lads being given a chance. They'd obviously been doing well to be in the squad. I didn't talk to them all that much. They tended to stick together. It was good they had come into the squad at the same time, not on their own as the youngest player.

They didn't make me feel like an old fart, even though I did have 29 caps under my belt. I hope everything goes well for them.

And it didn't make me look back at my life either, reminding me of what I've already done. I don't think like that. I don't look back or get emotional about things I've achieved.

My own England debut, yeah, that was good, I'll always remember it, but even at the time, I didn't get carried away. That's not me. And my Everton debut, that was good, hearing the strains of 'Z-cars' for the first time as I walked out, but really, I'd have to work hard to describe it to you.

Looking back, what did disappoint me was not making my Everton debut earlier. I would like to have got the record for the youngest-ever Everton player.

Of my three debuts, I suppose turning out for Man Utd was the best feeling. That did give me shivers down the spine. I was so proud to be a professional footballer, playing for the biggest club in England, walking out onto the biggest stage. And of course I did score a hat-trick. That has helped me remember it so well.

But generally, I have never gone around pinching myself, saying this is unbelievable, isn't it amazing what I'm doing or what I've done.

Some people have somehow got it into their heads that I've been an overnight success, come from nowhere, so I must be a bit stunned by all the things that have happened to me. That's not how I see it. All I see is ten years of hard work, of practising, and training, and discipline. It's been a long long time, all my life really, so I don't look around and think I'm dreaming.

Of course, it's fantastic playing for Man Utd, brilliant playing for England, but my main thought when I turn out for either of them is the same – I deserve it. That's what I'm thinking. I feel equal to the occasion. I've earned my place.

I suppose when I'm older, I might look back at it all a bit differently. I'll probably be more amazed in the future than I am now. All I can say now is that I'm living it, day to day, so I just accept it.

Off the pitch, I am a bit more aware of what has happened to me in the last four years. Often Coleen and I look around our big house, its six bedrooms and swimming pool, and think of where we have come from, of our life in our council houses. We haven't forgotten where we've come from.

We know we can buy anything we want. But what I don't like is people criticising footballers for how they spend their money. It's none of their business. I don't criticise other people about what they buy. But we do realise we are fortunate. We know there are millions not as lucky as we are.

I also know, as a footballer, I'm still learning, that's why I don't sit around thinking how well I've done. And I know there's a lot more to come in my career. Such as a World Cup, or so I hoped . . .

By joining the squad, I felt at least I was within touching distance of making it to the World Cup, but it turned out I wasn't quite as part of their routine as I'd hoped. While they went off in the England coach each day to training, I was driven in an FA car, on my own, because I had to go to a different part of Carrington for my training. I had to get on with my regime by myself, but I knew what they were doing on the training pitches, and was longing to join them.

It was very frustrating, not being able to train with my England team-mates, but I was soon doing a lot more running and some ball work, officially this time, under supervision. Naturally, I was soon thumping each ball as if I was playing in a World Cup Final.

I watched England's two friendlies at Old Trafford – which was horrible. I mean being forced to watch them, of course. The lads did well. the first game against Hungary was quite difficult, but we won 3–1, while the one against Jamaica was easier and ended in a 6–0 victory. I was delighted for Peter Crouch, getting his hat-trick. He's a nice lad but has had to put up with some unfair criticism earlier on.

His robot dance, after his hat-trick, was brilliant. We

all loved that, but we'd seen it before. He'd done it for us at Becks' pre-World Cup party.

I suppose the fact that he did so well took a bit of pressure off me. It gave the press something else to write about for a change.

The attention on me, during all my injury, was over the top, but I suppose in the weeks before a World Cup, the press are desperate for something to fill the pages. It was nice the nation was praying for me, so the papers said, willing me to play some part, but it did make it hard to carry on with my normal life, training and trying to relax, with all the fuss.

It didn't worry me that people would expect too much, that they were building me up when I was out, expecting I'd immediately perform miracles when I returned. Then perhaps they'd turn against me, if I wasn't as brilliant as they said I was going to be. I know I'll always do my best, whatever the circumstances. That's what matters.

Prince William came to see us all train one day. Apparently, he's taking on a role as president of the FA. He asked me about my foot, so I told him it was going well, I said I was hopeful of playing some part in the tournament, if I got through the next scan okay.

He seemed a nice bloke. He had a bit of banter with all the lads. He wasn't posh or stuck up, but he wasn't shy. All the lads egged on Crouchy to do his robot dance for him, which he did, so that was a good laugh.

The Scan

Before we finally left for Germany, there was the usual major event which I know the whole football world is always waiting for – the wearing of the World Cup suits.

Armani did them once again, and personally I thought they were much better this time. For Euro 2004, my suit had sort of flairs, and felt a bit baggy. This time it was a much tighter fit, which I like. I also liked the colour better – dark blue as opposed to grey green last time.

So, at last the squad was ready, fit and fitted out, to fly from Luton to Germany on 5 June. And I was with them, in the squad. But of course I still didn't know if I was ever going to make the team.

I was hardly there before I had to return to Manchester on 7 June, for the vital scan which would determine once and for all if I would make it.

The FA hired a special plane for me, which was kind. The team doctor, Leif Sward, came with me and so did David Davies from the FA. There was an FA security man as well. I was driven to the Whalley Range hospital and had the scan at about 12.30. It didn't take long, just around 45 minutes, with no retakes, which I thought was a good sign.

I was told they wouldn't be able to decide anything for about five hours, until all the doctors had had time to study the scan and think about it. So I went off to Coleen's, at her mum's house, and stayed there until about six o'clock. We just sat around, chatting, watching the telly.

245

Meanwhile, the experts got on with it. I don't know anything about any supposed arguments or differences of opinion amongst them. I wasn't aware of any, but then I wouldn't have been. I left it to them. As far as I was aware, there were five of them involved – two Manchester United doctors, the FA's doctor and two independent medical experts.

Eventually, I got called back, and was told that my foot had fully healed. It was absolutely brilliant news. I could now start full training. The only thing they warned me about was that I shouldn't think of playing before the Sweden game.

But Sven thought I might be fit to play some part in the Sweden game, and the FA doctor agreed. So the two independent experts might have to fly out to check me out first, to see if I was okay. I think that was the arrangement.

I wasn't really listening properly by then. All that concerned me was that the foot had healed. I was now ready to start training with the lads. At long last. I couldn't wait to get back on the plane to Germany.

By the time I arrived in Baden-Baden, the squad had already heard the news. And they too thought it was brilliant.

TWENTY-TWO

Germany Here I Come

Our hotel, the Schlosshotel Buhlerhohe, was outside Baden-Baden. It was in a very isolated situation, up a big hill, miles from anywhere, about fifteen minutes drive to the main town. It was very beautiful and luxurious, with very good medical facilities for a hotel, and huge grounds. Nelson Mandela had stayed there, so had Bill Clinton, and Oliver Kahn, the German goalie, got married there, so I was told.

The England squad, the players and all FA staff took over the whole hotel, so there were no other people staying there. It meant we had complete privacy, which was good. I liked it better than the hotel in Portugal for Euro 2004. That had more floors and we all got spread out a bit. This time, we were all closer together, mostly on the ground floor. I was in room 144, with Stevie Gerrard on one side and Frank Lampard on the other.

I had a bedroom and bathroom, TV and mini bar. No

alcohol in the mini bar of course, just water. My room was like most hotel rooms. No different really from the Lowry in Manchester. After a while, all hotel rooms seem much the same.

One good thing was the games room. It was enormous, with plenty of things to do, such as table tennis, snooker, and lots of video games and stuff. It was a bit like an amusement arcade. You didn't have to knock on someone's door, or ring them to say, 'Coming out to play?' You just had to go to the games room and you knew someone else would already be there. I liked the simulated golf game best.

Our training ground was only twenty minutes away and we went there each day by coach. From the very first day, I was doing full training with the rest of the squad, not on my own as I'd been doing in Manchester.

It was the normal sort of England training, from 10.15 until 12, same hours as at Man Utd. That's what all the players are used to.

The first 30 minutes involves tactical stuff, marking, working on our shape. Steve McClaren takes all this, while Sven usually watches. Then there's 30 minutes of a game, eleven-a-side. It's not a matter of the so-called first team against the second team. The coaches pick the teams. But as a match approaches, you begin to know from the set-piece work who'll be starting.

For the last 30 minutes or so, you can choose what to work on, such as passing or shooting. I always choose to do shooting. I do it from the edge of the penalty area, for 20 or 30 minutes.

There's normally no gym work with England, or weights, unless you're injured. It's assumed everybody arrives in good physical shape and doesn't need further conditioning. But I did some gym work as I was still getting up to match fitness. Luckily, during all the weeks out, I didn't put on weight.

From the first day of training in Germany, I was tackling hard – and being tackled hard. And when you get tackled by people like John Terry and Jamie Carragher, you know it. They didn't hold back. And neither did I. One of the papers said I went into Theo Walcott so hard he got injured, but this wasn't true. He did get a slight injury, but it wasn't as a result of my tackle.

After training each day, and then lunch, we would all go to our rooms to rest. Some people did sleep, but I couldn't manage it. I watched a series called *Lost* on DVD, part of a pile of stuff brought out for us. I had my own music, on my iPod, which I listened to a lot while travelling back and forth to training, stuff like Eminem and 50 Cent.

In the evening, after dinner, every one of the squad has a massage. This is one of Sven's ideas, which we don't do at Man Utd. There are three masseurs with the England team – Steve Slattery, Chris Neville and Rod Thornley – but it still takes a long time to do everyone. They normally take place from 7 until 10 pm. I always like to have mine as late as possible, about ten o'clock. I find I sleep better after a massage.

I read in the papers that the FA had brought a whole load of stuff specially for us, like 24 tons of Rice Krispies, 240 packets of Jaffa cakes, loads of porridge, acres of custard powder. I don't know where that all came from – or where it went. I didn't eat any of it. I wasn't asked to fill in any forms beforehand about my eating and drinking preferences. The FA must just have decided on their own what to bring for us, just in case anyone got homesick.

I ate as normal, just as I do at home. I don't have breakfast and I just have pasta or chicken for lunch and dinner. We had our own chef and he made us the stuff we normally eat.

About the only unusual thing that happened was that we each got a special letter from FIFA telling us not to bet on any of the World Cup games, whether we were involved in them or not. I know in previous World Cups the lads have often organised their own betting circles, betting on other games or watching videos of horse races and putting bets on amongst themselves. But there was none of that this time. I didn't do any betting, of any sort. Not after what happened last time . . .

There weren't any huge jokers in the England camp, not the way Gazza used to be, endlessly doing daft things, pushing people into the hotel pool and stuff. I'm about the only person who does silly things now. I might go up to people from behind and pull their pants down. Yes, pretty childish, but it amuses me. And everybody else seems to find it funny.

One of the many things we all enjoyed was watching the TV programme featuring Rio Ferdinand, the one where he played tricks on us, winding us up. We all had a laugh at ourselves.

On 10 June, in Frankfurt, England played their first game of the World Cup against Paraguay. As usual, we had all been shown a video of the opposition, and Sven went over their set-pieces, who would be doing what, who was supposed to mark who.

About two hours before kick-off, Sven always reads out the team, or at least confirms it, as we all know it by then. You can tell by the shape, and how we have been practising set-pieces. Usually it's already been decided two days ahead. I knew of course I wasn't in the starting line-up.

Before the lads go out, Sven always says the same thing. 'Go out and enjoy it.'

Kick-off was early afternoon and the heat was incredible. Even on the bench I was sweating. All the squad not playing sat on the bench, in our warm-up gear, because in theory any of us could come on as one of three subs. In the Premiership, you can only pick from five named subs. In this World Cup, anyone in the squad could come on.

For the first 30 minutes, the team did very well, and of course we got off to a good start with an early goal, the own goal, from Becks' free-kick. In the second half, we didn't seem to get going. I don't know why. The heat was part of the problem, and it did affect our performance, but you should never use heat as an excuse.

As the game wore on, and we started to tire, I was itching to come on. It was mad even thinking that, as Sven had made it clear beforehand to me that there was no chance of me playing. But all the same, I began to imagine I might be asked. Perhaps just before the end, he might change his mind? That's what was in my head. Especially when I could hear the crowd shouting my name, which was nice. Although, I think it was a good indication that I wouldn't play any part as I never warmed up.

After it was all over, I went out on the pitch with the other subs who hadn't played and we did a warm-down. I belted a ball into the goal from about thirty yards and all the England fans cheered. When we came off the field, I threw my training shirt into a crowd of England fans who'd been cheering me.

We'd won 1–0, not very convincingly, but it gave us three points and a great start. We would all have taken that result, if offered it, before kick-off.

After the match, the squad was told they would be having the next day and night off. The team who played got the whole day off but me and the other subs who hadn't played had to do some light training in the morning. Then we were free to do what we wanted.

It was great being able to see our girlfriends and wives and families. Sven always gives us time with them, unlike England managers in the past.

All of the wives and girlfriends had arrived the day before and were staying in Baden-Baden, at Brenner's Park Hotel. I had spoken to Coleen and she said the hotel was nice but they were getting hounded a bit. There were lots of other people staying there, including press, so they got watched and followed all the time. Behind the hotel was a very nice park, a public park, where people walk, so anyone could look over and see the girls sunbathing. When they went shopping in the town – which they did, being young girls – or had a few drinks, the press were continually snapping away, about a dozen British paps walking backwards in front of them. I think the locals were pretty stunned. It's a posh retirement town and they're not used to that sort of thing. Apparently, Clinton and Mandela didn't create anywhere near as much fuss as our girls did.

After training, on our day off, I went into town to meet Coleen. We had a walk about, and she gave me a present. It was a Rolex watch. On the back of it, she'd got it engraved 'To Wayne, Good Luck in the World Cup, Love Coleen.' So that was nice.

In the evening, she came back to our team hotel, as all the girls and wives did. They were allowed to stay the night, in our rooms. So that was good. As you can imagine . . .

For England's second game, against Trinidad & Tobago, I had arranged for my Mum and Dad and my two brothers, John and Graeme, to come out to watch it. Officially, I wasn't starting, or even supposed to be in line to come on as sub, but I got it into my head that this time I would be. Just little signs and nods from Sven that he thought I was now match-fit. Which was amazing, when you think about it, after only 45 days since my injury. Last time, it had taken twice as long, but that was a much more serious injury, on a different metatarsal.

I knew it would be difficult, and perhaps dangerous. Back in 2004 in Portugal, most of the foreign teams didn't really know me. Now they were all aware of me. I realised I was likely to get niggled more with opponents hoping to wind me up.

And of course they all knew about my injury. I had to expect some of them might even be trying to stand on my toes. But physically and mentally, I felt absolutely fine, raring to go. Desperate to make my first appearance in a World Cup . . .

TWENTY-THREE

On At Last

On the morning of the Trinidad & Tobago game, England's second in the World Cup, on 15 June in Nuremberg, the two independent medical experts flew out from England to check on my foot – and they said I was fine. The break had healed and I was now fit enough to be able to play, though not to start. Naturally I was delighted.

Before the match kicked off, Sven had told me I would be coming on, but I didn't know when. At half-time, when it was still 0–0, I could hear the crowd chanting my name as I was warming up on the pitch.

In the 52nd minute, I was brought on for Michael Owen. I felt fit enough, no fears at all. I didn't feel nervous or worried about being clattered or injured again, but my first touch was not good, not the way it should be. I was probably a bit ring rusty. But I was just so thrilled to be playing, to feel fit, back to normal.

Trinidad & Tobago were doing better than most

people had expected, and for a long time it didn't seem likely that we'd score, but my arrival did cheer up the crowd, and perhaps even the team. In the 82nd minute, Crouchy got a headed goal, then Stevie got an excellent one from outside the area in the 90th minute. So it ended 2–0 to us. We had done what we had set out to do, which was to win the match. I'd come on, at long last, and I'd finished the game, no bother, apart from not being as sharp as I would like to have been.

The next game, in Cologne on 20 June, was against Sweden, who'd been looked upon as our main rivals in the group. Sven told me well beforehand that I would be starting, along with Michael, so that was good. Now it did feel like I was back to normal.

I never read the English papers during the whole of the tournament. I don't normally read them anyway. Whatever the back pages might say doesn't really bother me, either way. But someone later told me that before that match I was reported as saying to the rest of the lads in the dressing room, 'The Big Man is Back'. That was rubbish. It's not me. I might have faults, but I'm not a big head. I presume it was just someone, somewhere, realising that after the Trinidad game I was now likely to start the next game – that I was 'back'. To make it better, they put the quote into my mouth – and got me all wrong. You can see why I don't read the papers.

A few minutes into the game, Michael went down,

injured. I didn't really see it, or take it in. I was following the ball. It was only when I noticed Crouchy warming up that I realised it was serious, but I still didn't know how bad it was. Perhaps some players did get a bit distracted for a moment, wondering what was going on.

It was only at half-time that Michael himself told us what had happened – his cruciate ligaments had gone. He would have to have an operation and could be out for months. It was a terrible blow for him. He'd worked so long and hard to get fit for the World Cup, far longer than me. It was tragic for him. We were all so upset on his behalf – and of course England's.

Fortunately, Joe Cole had scored a brilliant goal, a volley from miles out, so by the time we'd got to the dressing room at half-time and heard the news, we were 1–0 up and feeling confident.

I don't know what went wrong in the second half. Our defenders seemed to find themselves on the back foot. Sweden equalised from a corner and then a few minutes later they hit the crossbar. By then, we were struggling.

In the 68th minute, I got taken off. I was devastated. I was upset by my own display, at how the team were playing, and at Sven for taking me off. All three reasons, really. We never got out of first gear.

When I got to the bench, I gave the side of the dug-out a kicking. Then when I took my boots off, I threw them down on the ground in disgust.

At the time you are doing these daft things you are not really aware of the fact millions of people round the world are watching you. You don't think about it, and you don't care. It's just the same as when I'm playing in front of nobody in a training game at Carrington. You get wound up, so you show your feelings.

When Gary Neville, who was injured and not playing, leaned over to me in the dug-out, everyone presumed he was telling me off for throwing my boots down in a temper. Or at least that he was telling me to calm down.

In fact, all he said was, 'Keep drinking the liquids', which made sense. We all know that when you come off, you should take as much fluid as you can, because while on the pitch the body gets dehydrated. He did apparently smile when he said it, knowing he was partly teasing me, knowing I had a cob on. I didn't actually see his smile. I was blanking him and the whole world. I was just so upset not to be on the pitch playing my heart out.

Stevie Gerrard headed a goal in the 84th minute to make it 2–1 to us, but we still seemed to be struggling with set-pieces. In the 89th minute, Henrik Larsson managed to squeeze the ball in after a long throw-in. So the game ended 2–2.

We'd finished top of the group, so that was good, even though we hadn't been on great form. Afterwards, Sven said nothing to me personally. He hadn't of course seen me throwing my boots down. I didn't moan or complain about being taken off. I felt I was fit enough, could have played longer, but I knew I hadn't been doing brilliantly. That was what had upset me, more than Sven taking me off. However, we were all well pleased to be through to the last 16.

Although I didn't read the English newspapers, we all picked up from the wives and girlfriends that the press were having a constant go at us for not being good enough. Normally it washes over you, but this time we did get a bit upset by the criticism.

Okay, so we didn't play as well as we could, as we would have liked, but nobody seemed to be giving us praise for coming top of the group. How could we have done better than that? All we seemed to be getting was a hammering.

The papers were also being horrible about the wives and girlfriends, saying they should never have been allowed near us – in his day Alf Ramsay would not have let them – and that they were just a distraction. I disagreed. We only ever saw them on the day after a game, not every day as some people seemed to believe. I think they were a positive help, especially for the players with kids. It was great for them to see their children. Otherwise they would have been apart from them for four or five weeks. It did help the players relax, feel settled, ease the tension.

I know the papers went on about the girls going out

on the town, singing and drinking champagne, but what we didn't read about was some of the journalists drinking each night, and getting hammered. I can tell you the name of one, because Coleen saw him, drunk in her hotel, plus some others. After rubbishing the girls for having a few drinks, they themselves went out and got slaughtered. She also heard one of them singing a disgusting and obscene anti-Liverpool song. None of that made the papers.

During the World Cup, we had to travel in a FIFA coach, not our own England one. It was okay, we didn't usually have to go too far for each game. I just listened to my iPod, or texted my friends. Our own hotel became like home in the end. Time did drag now and again, so that was why it was great seeing the wives and girlfriends. I didn't really get bored. It was more a case of wanting the next game to hurry up. I couldn't wait to play each time.

Gary Neville spared us one of his guitar recitals, thank God. Actually, he's quite good. He's been learning the guitar for a few years now. He took it with him but he never played it in front of the squad as far as I know. I think he just practised in his room. It's a good idea, I suppose. It gave him something to do. If I had hobbies, I might do the same. At the moment, my only hobby is er, let me think, football – and sleeping. I wonder what I might take up in the years to come. Chess? Rocket science? Or I could go back to RE, at which I used to be excellent.

In the lead-up to each game, we had to spend the night before in a city centre hotel, organised by FIFA, not our own FA. This was to make sure we arrived at the stadiums on time. Sometimes these hotels can be really noisy and horrible, compared with our usual luxury, five-star places out in the country with massive grounds, peace and quiet. They all turned out fine though. I had no problems. I slept well, on the whole.

In the hotel they gave us in Frankfurt, before the Trinidad & Tobago match, there was a very good massage room. It was huge, well equipped, and on the ground floor. I was sitting there, being massaged, not long after we arrived, and I happened to look up through one of the windows. I didn't quite know where I was at the time, I mean where the room was in the hotel, until I suddenly realised I could see straight out onto the street – and there outside were a dozen or so England fans, walking up and down, singing and shouting.

I shouted to some of the lads, 'Hey, come and look at this,' and so they did, joining me to look out through the window. One of the fans outside recognized me, and at once he started shouting my name. '*Roonee, Roonee . . .*' Very soon, all the others joined in, and then more appeared from nowhere, all singing my name, and the names of the other players, plus all the Ingerland songs. In the end, there must have been about

3,000 England fans outside that window, shouting and singing.

We all waved back at them, and sang some of the songs. The players loved it, pleased to hear the supporters shouting for us, proud of the support. In fact quite a few of the players were saying that they would have liked to have been out there with them, singing in the street, walking about with their mates, having a few beers. I would definitely have enjoyed it. That's all to come, of course, when we finish playing football. I'll still be a football fan, whatever happens to me in the future, just as all my family have always been.

Throughout the World Cup, the England supporters were brilliant. They were also well behaved, whatever some of the press might have been saying beforehand. It was great to hear them singing and cheering when we walked out on to the pitch and then all the way through our games, even if we were not exactly playing brilliant all the time. Their support was positive and genuine. They did help, unlike some of the football reporters . . .

So we'd got to the final sixteen, the first of the knock-out stages. We were to play Ecuador in Stuttgart on 25 June.

Just before our pre-match meal, when we were sitting in the hotel dining room waiting for food to be served, Sven called me aside. He asked if he could have a few words with me, on my own, in private. He did it discreetly, so no one was aware of what was happening.

I followed him out of the dining room, towards a balcony of the hotel. He was obviously going to take me out onto this balcony, close the door behind us, then tell me one-to-one whatever it was he was going to say.

Either he wasn't concentrating or didn't yet know his way round this hotel as he thought he did, but he walked straight into a plate glass window, giving himself a really nasty smack. He must have thought it was an open door.

For about ten minutes I laughed like a drain, even when he was into what he wanted to tell me. I don't think he was at all amused. Embarrassed, really, and a bit bruised.

What he had to say to me was – would I be prepared to play up front on my own against Ecuador? To be honest, as I've told you, I do prefer to play as the second striker, just behind the main front man. That's where I think I'm happiest and can do my best work, contribute most to the team. I'm sure Sven knew that. I didn't need to tell him. He's seen me play enough times. So I didn't argue or point it out.

'No problems, boss,' I said. 'If that's where you want me to play, for the good of the team, I'll do it, don't worry.'

Obviously he'd worked it out that with Michael injured and out of the tournament, I was the best person to be up front on my own for this match.

If it had been my decision, I would probably have preferred Crouchy up front, with me behind, but it wasn't my shout. You have to believe the manager knows best. Which I did. I had complete trust in him, that he was doing the best thing in the circumstances.

People later said it was a mistake, or a big risk, giving me all that responsibility and burden, because I'd never played there before, all on my own, up front. But that's not quite correct. During my first season with Man Utd, I played up front on my own eight times. Giggsy was on one wing, Ronaldo on the other, but I was up front in the middle on my own. Yes, it wasn't exactly the same as the England formation, but near enough. Against Ecuador, Joe Cole was playing in an advanced position on one side of me, and Becks on the other. So it came to the same thing.

In the warm-up before the game, I found myself beside Becks.

'You're gonna score from a free-kick today,' I said to him.

'How do you know?' he asked me.

I laughed. 'Because your free-kicks have been s**t in training all week.'

And what happened? He scored from a brilliant free-kick in the 60th minute.

In the first half I hadn't played all that well, but in the second half I felt myself getting stronger, more confident. Perhaps it had to do with getting used to the position. I had a couple of good runs, beat a few players. I managed to nutmeg a defender near the bye-line, moved in towards the goal and got in a good cross to Lamps, giving him a chance to score, but unfortunately it didn't quite work out on this occasion.

I finished the ninety minutes feeling really good. I knew I'd got better as the game progressed – and was getting better in every match. I'd now had three games, so any slowness or hangover from the metatarsal had well and truly gone. I was well match-fit.

We won 1–0, thanks to Becks's free-kick, and were now into the quarter-finals, despite what some of the papers had predicted.

Okay, we hadn't set the World Cup finals alight, not so far. But everything we'd hoped and planned for had come to pass. We all felt sure the best was to come . . .

TWENTY-FOUR

Red-Carded

Our quarter-final game took place on 1 July in Gelsen-kirchen against Portugal – old friends and old rivals of mine, and of England's. Each of my two metatarsal injuries had occurred against a Portuguese player, but I'm not talking about that anymore. It's history, gone from my mind.

I suppose it was quite a good draw. We had avoided Germany, the host country, who were playing better and better. They were drawn against Argentina, so one of them would go out, while Brazil was playing France in another quarter-final. It meant that by the semi-finals, whatever happened, some really good teams would be on the way home, leaving things a bit easier for the ones left. In theory anyway.

We fully expected to be in the semi-finals. We felt we'd been the equal of Portugal in Euro 2004, when I'd got injured and we'd only gone out on penalties. This time we believed it was our turn to come out on top. We knew so far we hadn't performed as we knew we could, but we really were confident, sure we were going to get better and better as the competition progressed.

I'd be playing against Cristiano Ronaldo, which I was looking forward to. It had been doubtful whether he'd play, because of an injury, but we heard not long before the match that he was fit. I was pleased for him. No one wants to miss the chance of appearing in a World Cup game.

Ronny's a good friend of mine. At Man Utd, we're usually the two youngest in the squad, so we often partner each other in training, and have a few laughs together.

As we came down the tunnel and went out onto the pitch, me and Ronny had a bit of banter together. Most commentators, and most people watching on TV back home, thought Ronny was winding me up. Especially in the light of what happened afterwards. They imagined he was saying, 'You're going to get stuffed today, we're going to thump you!' That is the sort of thing friends say to each other before a match, any sort of match, even a World Cup one, just as a joke, a bit of friendly banter. No one takes it seriously. But on this occasion, Ronny didn't say that.

Some people maintained later that they could read his lips and what he was saying was a threat: 'I'm going to get you sent off today.'

That's because I was looking serious while he was

sort of smirking and sniggering, while giving me a little poke on the back of my shoulder. But that's how I always look before going onto the pitch. I try to stay serious and focused.

What we really talked about might come as a bit of a shock to some people – because it was so boring. Hardly worth repeating really, if so many hadn't got it all wrong.

First of all, in the tunnel, we wished each other good luck in the game, hoped it went well, which is what you always say to team-mates. Okay, he wasn't in my team that day, but you still wish a fellow professional to have a good game.

Then he asked me if I'd heard where Quinton Fortune was going. I said no, did he know where he was going?

Quinton's a friend and club mate of both of us and he was reported to be leaving Man Utd. Neither of us knew the latest. So that was it. We said good luck to each other, once more. And then the game began.

I was playing up front again, on my own. Sven decided I had done a decent job against Ecuador, and had got stronger and better as the game went on. Gary Neville had recovered from injury and returned to right-back, so we were all pleased by that. Owen Hargreaves was moved into the middle, in place of Michael Carrick, which was hard luck on him, to sit in front of our defence.

In the first minute, I managed a shot on goal, which pleased me, even though it didn't go in. A few minutes later I managed another break. Then we sort of settled down, with neither side dominating or playing very well. We weren't at our best, nor was I. I failed to control the ball once or twice when normally I would have, but I wasn't too worried. I thought we were slowly beginning to control the game and would win, because they were doing nothing much. At half-time it was 0–0.

Five minutes into the second half, Becks had to come off injured and Aaron Lennon replaced him. He did really well, livened things up, and I felt I was getting better.

In the 58th minute I missed a good chance in front of goal. The ball came across to me suddenly. I scratched at it with my left leg and it went wide. I'd rushed it, and ruined the chance. But I wasn't too bothered or frustrated. I felt I was playing well, the team was getting better, so we'd do it in the end.

Just around the hour mark, a ball was played up to me near the centre circle. I managed to control it but at once three Portuguese players surrounded me, with two of them pushing and shoving, trying to get the ball off me. I was still struggling to control the ball, twisting and turning, trying to keep them off, in order to give myself space to do something, but they clung on.

One player slid into me, and he fell down, which I thought was a foul on me. The other knocked me in the back, so I fell over. I lost my balance and landed on the fella on the ground.

The ref blew and I honestly thought I was going to be awarded a free-kick. Each of them had fouled me, so I thought, in trying to get the ball off me. By this time, Ronny had run up, though it was nothing to do with him, he hadn't been involved in the incident. He appeared to be telling the ref I should get a card. And then to my amazement the ref was putting his hand up in the air. With a red card. For me. I was off. All I felt was disbelief.

In being forced back, I had trod on the player on the ground, I realised that. It turned out to be Ricardo Carvalho of Chelsea. And I was aware that my foot had landed between his legs, which of course is about the nastiest place to get hurt, but it was an accident. I couldn't believe that the ref, who was so near, hadn't realised that. Perhaps he was too near. What he saw, close up, was the player on the ground and then my foot going into his groin.

I'll go to my grave and still maintain it was a complete accident. I hadn't intended to do it. If you study the photographs, you'll see that when I fell I had my back to the player. I couldn't see him, or where I was putting my foot.

If you think about it, if I'd done it deliberately, if it had been a definite stamp meant to harm him, the fella would still be in hospital to this day. But he was up on his feet in minutes, no worse for wear. Obviously it hadn't been pleasant for him, but it was all an accident, the sort of thing that happens when you are fighting hard for the ball.

However, the ref saw it differently. He saw it as violent play – and I was off. I was disappointed by Ronny, trying to get me carded, and I gave him a bit of a push in the chest. But that was it.

I couldn't bear to sit on the bench and watch so I went straight to the dressing room accompanied by Slats, one of the England physios.

There was a TV in the dressing room, showing the game, so we just sat and watched the rest of it together. In silence. I didn't want to speak to anyone. I was still gutted, shocked, unable to believe what had happened. I was too angry to cry.

I watched the lads doing brilliantly. Crouchy had come on after I'd got sent off. He was up front on his own, while poor old Joe Cole had had to come off. I thought Crouchy was doing excellently and Owen Hargreaves was amazing, working so hard and so well.

After 90 minutes it was still 0–0, so it went to extra-time. At the end of extra-time, still goalless, it meant England had played for an hour with only ten men. I felt they had finished the better team. In fact towards the end of extra-time they had chances from a couple of corners to have won. They deserved to, I thought. I wouldn't have played in the semis, but I'd be available for the final, if we made it.

But we blew it on penalties, once again. We missed three out of our four. And that was it.

I don't blame any of the penalty-takers. You can practise all you like in training and we had, throughout the tournament, but it's never the same as real life. You just don't know what will have gone before and how everyone will feel at the time.

If I'd been on the pitch, I would have taken one of the penalties. Probably the first one. Would I have scored? Who knows. A penalty is always 50–50. But I am always confident I'll score.

The second it finished, I had a shower and got changed. The lads were still out on the pitch, absolutely knackered, shattered, most of them lying down, unable to move. Gary Neville, who had ended the match as captain, did do the right thing. He went round and congratulated the Portuguese.

Then slowly all the England lads trooped in, in silence. I was sitting on the bench, sad and depressed, rather than angry. I'd got over my raging fury.

They came over to me, one by one, said things like 'Don't worry, Wazza, it wasn't your fault . . . don't be too upset.'

That was when, for the first time, I felt a few tears come into my eyes. I don't cry often. And I hadn't cried when I'd been sent off. Having got over my own anger, I was beginning to feel sad – this time for them, rather than myself. I didn't feel guilty about what had happened, because I still felt innocent. But my sending off had let them down. Because of me, for whatever reason, they'd been made to struggle on with only ten men.

Sven came over to me, just to ask what happened. He wasn't angry with me, he didn't give me a bollocking. I told him my version of the incident, how I hadn't meant it. He listened to me quietly and when I'd finished he said, 'These things happen.'

On the coach to Baden-Baden, it was like there had been a death. All the players were shattered, disappointed, devastated.

They had tried to cheer me up back in the dressing room, so this time, on the coach, I went round them, telling them how well they'd done, that all of them had tried their best. I was proud of them, as everyone should be of themselves. They had deserved to win. Portugal had not been the better team. Just lucky on penalties.

So, that was it. England's 2006 World Cup dream was over – and mine too.

Next morning, I left the team hotel early and went straight into town to Coleen's hotel. I was still upset and sad, I didn't really want to talk about it, or to meet people. Coleen was brilliant. She calmed me down, said it wasn't my fault, I couldn't have helped it. I just had to look forward not back.

I was no longer angry over what had happened, or

even with Ronny. It seemed that the papers were trying to stir it up, rubbishing him, blaming him.

They reported that after the game, while I was still in our dressing room, I had tried to get into the Portuguese dressing room, in order to hit Ronny. That's not true. By then, such a thought wasn't even going through my mind.

What the papers didn't know, and probably will never believe, is that on the coach, on the way home after the game, I sent a text to Ronny. I told him to forget about what happened. I wasn't blaming him for interfering. Then I wished him and Portugal good luck in the semis and hoped they got to the final. And I meant it.

I'd like to think I don't do things like diving and making a meal of every contact, the way some players did at the World Cup. Before that red card incident, I could have gone down, after that first tackle, rolled around on the ground, perhaps got a foul, or even the other bloke carded. But I didn't because my only aim was to stay on my feet and keep the ball, not gain an advantage.

But the players do try it. By protesting to the ref, Ronny was doing what he thought was good for his country.

During that game, we were rivals, which was why I gave him a push when I thought he'd been out of order. But once it was all over, we were friends, club mates again. It was all forgotten.

On the BBC studio panel, Alan Shearer said that when

Red-Carded

I met up with Ronny again in training, I should 'stick one on him.' I think Alan said that in the heat of the moment. England had just been knocked out and he was choked, as we all were. But I never thought like that, not once it was all over.

Another paper said I was going to have anger management therapy. They even named a Manchester woman I had gone to, and was going to see again, so they said. It was all rubbish. I've never seen such a person, and never would.

Other papers said I was a disgrace, I'd behaved like a thug. Well, that's their opinion. But it's all wrong. As I've told you, standing on Carvalho was a total accident.

As for being angry, I might get upset and frustrated during a game, often by myself rather than other people, but it's only because I want to win so much. Off the pitch, I don't get angry. I never bear grudges. I'm not vindictive. I don't have a list of players I want to get my own back on, which I know some players do. I don't have people I don't like, in or outside football.

I suppose I'm laid back. I don't get bothered, either way, by what people do or say. All I care about in life is being out there, playing football – and of course Coleen. That's about it really.

But what happens is that people look at you, and at how I happen to look, especially when I'm out there on the pitch, and they imagine they know your character.

But they don't. Me, in real life, I think I'm a quiet, sensitive, retiring, shy person. That's my image of myself.

Some so-called experts have said that my anger on the pitch, resulting in the red card, was all Sven's fault. I had been forced into a role, given too much responsibility. I would have helped the team more as a second striker, in my usual position, working alongside Peter Crouch. In that case, I might not have had three defenders round me all the time, and not got so frustrated. But I didn't personally feel frustrated. I think it could have happened at any time, in any match.

As I've said, I agreed to do it. Sven wanted to pack the midfield. We all knew and understood, that was our plan. I didn't moan about it – and now it's long over, I'm not complaining. It seemed right at the time.

Even now, I have not changed my mind about Sven. I thought he was good for England, at the time. So why didn't we do as well as we should have done? You tell me. I don't know the exact reasons. The heat? Michael being injured? Bad refereeing decisions. If I knew the answers, I'd be a brilliant manager. Perhaps we did get nervous towards the end. The tension could have got to us, people watching might have thought that, but we honestly weren't aware of it. I believed as a team we were all confident of coming good. I know I was.

Sir Alex rang me afterwards, to commiserate and to

see how I felt. He told me not to worry too much about the red card. But I hadn't. It was already history.

I was a bit surprised by Becks when he announced he was resigning as captain. I didn't know he was going to say that. But he was as devastated as we all were by what happened. I'm sure Stevie or John Terry will make excellent captains.

Could I be captain one day? You never know. I like to feel I can be a leader on the pitch, urge on the lads, even if my example is not always the best, but I am getting better. I was captain of the Everton team that got to the Youth Cup Final in 2002.

I was pleased Italy won the World Cup, but a bit surprised. I didn't watch all the games, as we were playing, or travelling or training, but I thought Argentina looked about the best team.

When I look back at the World Cup in 2006, I don't actually see it as a bad or unhappy time. I just feel happy and privileged that I appeared for England in a World Cup. It was a great event for me. People say 'Oh, he'll now learn by it, by what happened to him, he'll be wiser in the future.' That doesn't always follow. What I've had is the experience, and so that must help me in the future.

As soon as it was all over, I started planning a holiday with Coleen. We decided to hire a private luxury yacht and went cruising in the Med off the South of France. We didn't fancy a hotel as it would result in a lot of hassle from the press. Anyway, I'd had enough of hotels by then.

We did think about inviting some of the family, as we usually do on our hols, like the cousins, Coleen's mum and dad, all our close relations. That could have been a laugh.

Just five years ago, I was going on my hols with all the Rooneys, hiring our own coach to go to Butlins. It would have been quite a change for all of us to have been on a luxury yacht, with a full staff, sailing into St Tropez or Monte Carlo or wherever. Could have been fun, though we might also have needed a few bouncers . . .

In the end, it was just me and Coleen and a few friends.

What I am focused on now is the season ahead. I'm already looking forward to it. The vital thing is that Chelsea don't win the Premiership for a third time. That would be horrible. So this new season is massive for Man Utd and it's vital we get off to a good start.

Chelsea have got several new world-class players, but on the other hand it always takes time for new players to settle in. It's not necessarily a huge advantage for them. We are more settled, and getting better all the time.

We don't actually look upon Chelsea as our main rivals – that's still Liverpool, followed by Man City. I'd personally rather beat Liverpool than Chelsea.

Naturally, because of where I come from and how my career began, I always look for Everton's result. And I always will, but I no longer feel for them as I did. When we play them, I want to win, and the three points are sweeter because it's Everton. It's a weird feeling. Too much happened before and during my transfer for me to ever feel the same.

I am still grateful for what they did when I was in their Academy. I would say that Colin Harvey has still been the biggest single influence on my career. He pushed me hard when he took over the Academy, made me more aware as a player, made me believe in myself. And of course I have to be grateful to David Moyes, for giving me my chance to play in the Premiership. That all seems quite a long time ago. Now I've got a World Cup behind me, when for so long I never thought I would, I have a lot to look forward to. Such as another four World Cups . . .

APPENDIX ONE

Club Career

For EVERTON 2002–03

Date	Competition	Opponents	Venue	Result	Rooney Goals
17.08.02	PL	Tottenham Hotspur	Goodison Park	D 2–2	–
24.08.02	PL	Sunderland	Stadium of Light	W 1–0	–
28.08.02	PL	Birmingham City	Goodison Park	D 1–1	–
31.08.02	PL	Manchester City	Maine Road	L 1–3	–
11.09.02	PL	Southampton	St Mary's	L 1–2	–
14.09.02	PL	Middlesbrough	Goodison Park	W 2–1	–
22.09.02	PL	Aston Villa	Villa Park	L 2–3	–
01.10.02	LC	Wrexham	Racecourse Ground	W 3–0	2
07.10.02	PL	Manchester United	Old Trafford	L 0–3	–
19.10.02	PL	Arsenal	Goodison Park	W 2–1	1
27.10.02	PL	West Ham United	Upton Park	W 1–0	–
03.11.02	PL	Leeds United	Elland Road	W 1–0	1
06.11.02	LC	Newcastle United	St James' Park	D 3–3	–
09.11.02	PL	Charlton Athletic	Goodison Park	W 1–0	–
17.11.02	PL	Blackburn Rovers	Ewood Park	W 1–0	–
23.11.02	PL	West Bromwich Albion	Goodison Park	W 1–0	–
01.12.02	PL	Newcastle United	St James' Park	L 1–2	–
04.12.02	LC	Chelsea	Stamford Bridge	L 1–4	–
07.12.02	PL	Chelsea	Goodison Park	L 1–3	–
14.12.02	PL	Blackburn Rovers	Goodison Park	W 2–1	1
22.12.02	PL	Liverpool	Anfield	D 0–0	–

Date	Competition	Opponents	Venue	Result	Rooney Goals
26.12.02	PL	Birmingham City	St Andrews	D 1–1	–
28.12.02	PL	Bolton Wanderers	Goodison Park	D 0–0	–
01.01.03	PL	Manchester City	Goodison Park	D 2–2	–
04.01.03	FAC	Shrewsbury Town	Gay Meadow	L 1–2	–
08.02.03	PL	Charlton Athletic	The Valley	L 1–2	–
22.02.03	PL	Southampton	Goodison Park	W 2–1	–
01.03.03	PL	Middlesbrough	Riverside Stadium	D 1–1	–
15.03.03	PL	West Ham United	Goodison Park	D 0–0	–
23.03.03	PL	Arsenal	Highbury	L 1–2	1
06.04.03	PL	Newcastle United	Goodison Park	W 2–1	1
12.04.03	PL	West Bromwich Albion	The Hawthorns	W 2–1	–
19.04.03	PL	Liverpool	Goodison Park	L 1–2	–
21.04.03	PL	Chelsea	Stamford Bridge	L 1–4	–
26.04.03	PL	Aston Villa	Goodison Park	W 2–1	1
03.05.03	PL	Fulham	Loftus Road	L 0–2	–
11.05.03	PL	Manchester United	Goodison Park	L 1–2	–

Total games played = 14 (+19 as sub)
Total goals scored = 6 in the League, +2 in Cup

KEY: PL = PREMIER LEAGUE;   LC = LEAGUE CUP;   FAC = FA CUP

For EVERTON 2003–04

Date	Competition	Opponents	Venue	Result	Rooney Goals
16.08.03	PL	Arsenal	Highbury	L 1–2	–
23.08.03	PL	Fulham	Goodison Park	W 3–1	–
26.08.03	PL	Charlton Athletic	The Valley	D 2–2	1
30.08.03	PL	Liverpool	Goodison Park	L 0–3	–
13.09.03	PL	Newcastle United	Goodison Park	D 2–2	–
21.09.03	PL	Middlesbrough	Riverside Stadium	L 0–1	–
24.09.03	LC	Stockport County	Goodison Park	W 3–0	–
28.09.03	PL	Leeds United	Goodison Park	W 4–0	–
04.10.03	PL	Tottenham Hotspur	White Hart Lane	L 0–3	–
25.10.03	PL	Aston Villa	Villa Park	D 0–0	–

Club Career

Date	Competition	Opponents	Venue	Result	Rooney Goals
29.10.03	LC	Charlton Athletic	Goodison Park	W 1–0	–
01.11.03	PL	Chelsea	Goodison Park	L 1–0	–
22.11.03	PL	Wolves	Goodison Park	W 2–0	–
29.11.03	PL	Bolton Wanderers	Reebok Stadium	L 0–2	–
03.12.03	LC	Middlesbrough	Riverside Stadium	D 0–0	–
07.12.03	PL	Manchester City	Goodison Park	D 0–0	–
13.12.03	PL	Portsmouth	Fratton Park	W 2–1	1
20.12.03	PL	Leicester City	Goodison Park	W 3–2	1
26.12.03	PL	Manchester United	Old Trafford	L 2–3	–
28.12.03	PL	Birmingham City	Goodison Park	W 1–0	1
03.01.04	FAC	Norwich City	Goodison Park	W 3–1	–
07.01.04	PL	Arsenal	Goodison Park	D 1–1	–
10.01.04	PL	Fulham	Loftus Road	L 1–2	–
17.01.04	PL	Charlton Athletic	Goodison Park	L 0–1	–
25.01.04	FAC	Fulham	Goodison Park	D 1–1	–
31.01.04	PL	Liverpool	Anfield	D 0–0	–
04.02.04	FAC	Fulham	Loftus Road	L 1–2	–
07.02.04	PL	Manchester United	Goodison Park	L 3–4	–
11.02.04	PL	Birmingham City	St Andrews	L 0–3	–
21.02.04	PL	Southampton	St Mary's	D 3–3	2
28.02.04	PL	Aston Villa	Goodison Park	W 2–0	–
13.03.04	PL	Portsmouth	Goodison Park	W 1–0	1
20.03.04	PL	Leicester City	Walkers Stadium	D 1–1	1
27.03.04	PL	Middlesbrough	Goodison Park	D 1–1	–
13.04.04	PL	Leeds United	Elland Road	D 1–1	1
17.04.04	PL	Chelsea	Stamford Bridge	D 0–0	–
24.04.04	PL	Blackburn Rovers	Goodison Park	L 0–1	–
01.05.04	PL	Wolves	Molineux	L 1–2	–
08.05.04	PL	Bolton Wanderers	Goodison Park	L 1–2	–
15.05.04	PL	Manchester City	City of Manchester	L 1–5	–

Total games played = 26 (+8 as sub)
Total goals scored = 9 in league

KEY: PL = PREMIER LEAGUE;   LC = LEAGUE CUP;   FAC = FA CUP

For MANCHESTER UNITED 2004–05

Date	Competition	Opponents	Venue	Result	Rooney Goals
28.09.04	ECLQ	Fenerbahçe	Old Trafford	W 6–2	3
03.10.04	PL	Middlesbrough	Old Trafford	D 1–1	–
16.10.04	PL	Birmingham City	St Andrews	D 0–0	–
19.10.04	ECL	Sparta Prague	Prague	D 0–0	–
24.10.04	PL	Arsenal	Old Trafford	W 2–0	1
30.10.04	PL	Portsmouth	Fratton Park	L 0–2	–
03.11.04	EC	Sparta Prague	Old Trafford	W 4–1	–
07.11.04	PL	Manchester City	Old Trafford	D 0–0	–
14.11.04	PL	Newcastle United	St James' Park	W 3–1	2
20.11.04	PL	Charlton Athletic	Old Trafford	W 2–0	–
23.11.04	ECL	Lyons	Old Trafford	W 2–1	–
27.11.04	PL	West Bromwich Albion	The Hawthorns	W 3–0	–
04.12.04	PL	Southampton	Old Trafford	W 3–0	1
13.12.04	PL	Fulham	Craven Cottage	D 1–1	–
18.12.04	PL	Crystal Palace	Old Trafford	W 5–2	–
26.12.04	PL	Bolton Wanderers	Old Trafford	W 2–0	–
28.12.04	PL	Aston Villa	Villa Park	W 1–0	–
12.01.05	LC	Chelsea	Stamford Bridge	D 0–0	–
15.01.05	PL	Liverpool	Anfield	W 1–0	1
19.01.05	FAC	Exeter City	St James' Park	W 2–0	1
22.01.05	PL	Aston Villa	Old Trafford	W 3–1	–
26.01.05	LC	Chelsea	Old Trafford	L 1–2	–
29.01.05	FAC	Middlesbrough	Old Trafford	W 3–0	2
01.02.05	PL	Arsenal	Highbury	W 4–2	–
05.02.05	PL	Birmingham City	Old Trafford	W 2–0	1
13.02.05	PL	Manchester City	City of Manchester	W 2–0	1
19.02.05	FAC	Everton	Goodison Park	W 2–0	–
23.02.05	ECL	AC Milan	Old Trafford	L 1–0	–
26.02.05	PL	Portsmouth	Old Trafford	W 2–1	2
05.03.05	PL	Crystal Palace	Selhurst Park	D 0–0	–
08.03.05	ECL	AC Milan	San Siro	L 0–1	–
12.03.05	FAC	Southampton	St Mary's	W 4–0	–
19.03.05	PL	Fulham	Old Trafford	W 1–0	–
02.04.05	PL	Blackburn Rovers	Old Trafford	D 0–0	–
09.04.05	PL	Norwich City	Carrow Road	L 0–2	–

Club Career

Date	Competition	Opponents	Venue	Result	Rooney Goals
17.04.05	FAC	Newcastle	St James' Park	W 4–1	–
20.04.05	PL	Everton	Goodison Park	L 0–1	–
24.04.05	PL	Newcastle	Old Trafford	W 2–1	1
01.05.05	PL	Charlton	The Valley	W 4–0	1
07.05.05	PL	West Bromwich Albion	Old Trafford	D 1–1	–
10.05.05	PL	Chelsea	Old Trafford	L 1–3	–
15.05.05	PL	Southampton	St Mary's	W 2–1	–
21.05.05	FAC	Arsenal	Millennium Stadium	D 0–0*	–

Total games played = 24 (+5 as sub)

Total goals scored = 11 in League, 6 in Cups

KEY: PL = PREMIER LEAGUE;   LC = LEAGUE CUP;   FAC = FA CUP;
ECLQ = EUROPEAN CHAMPIONS LEAGUE QUALIFIER; ECL = EUROPEAN
CHAMPIONS LEAGUE.

(*Arsenal won on penalties)

For MANCHESTER UNITED 2005–06

Date	Competition	Opponents	Venue	Result	Rooney Goals
09.08.05	ECLQ	Debreceni	Old Trafford	W 3–0	1
13.08.05	PL	Everton	Goodison Park	W 2–0	1
20.08.05	PL	Aston Villa	Old Trafford	W 1–0	–
28.08.05	PL	Newcastle	St James' Park	W 2–0	1
10.09.05	PL	Manchester City	Old Trafford	D 1–1	–
14.09.05	ECL	Villarreal	Mestalla	D 0–0	–
18.09.05	PL	Liverpool	Anfield	D 0–0	–
24.09.05	PL	Blackburn	Old Trafford	L 1–2	–
01.10.05	PL	Fulham	Craven Cottage	W 3–2	1
15.10.05	PL	Sunderland	Stadium of Light	W 3–1	1
22.10.05	PL	Tottenham Hotspur	Old Trafford	D 1–1	–
29.10.05	PL	Middlesbrough	Riverside Stadium	L 1–4	–
02.11.05	ECL	Lille	Lille Stadium	L 0–1	–
06.11.05	PL	Chelsea	Old Trafford	W 1–0	–
19.11.05	PL	Charlton	The Valley	W 3–1	–
22.11.05	ECL	Villarreal	Old Trafford	D 0–0	–
27.11.05	PL	West Ham United	Upton Park	W 2–1	1

Wayne Rooney: My Story So Far

Date	Competition	Opponents	Venue	Result	Rooney Goals
03.12.05	PL	Portsmouth	Old Trafford	W 3–0	1
07.12.05	ECL	Benfica	Stadium of Light	L 1–2	–
11.12.05	PL	Everton	Old Trafford	D 1–1	–
14.12.05	PL	Wigan Athletic	Old Trafford	W 4–0	2
17.12.05	PL	Aston Villa	Villa Park	W 2–0	–
20.12.05	LC	Birmingham City	St Andrews	W 3–1	–
26.12.05	PL	West Bromwich Albion	Old Trafford	W 3–0	–
28.12.05	PL	Birmingham City	St Andrews	D 2–2	–
31.12.05	PL	Bolton Wanderers	Old Trafford	W 4–1	–
03.01.06	PL	Arsenal	Highbury	D 0–0	–
08.01.06	FAC	Burton Albion	Pirelli Stadium	D 0–0	–
11.01.06	LC	Blackburn Rovers	Ewood Park	D 1–1	–
14.01.06	PL	Manchester City	City of Manchester	L 1–3	–
22.01.06	PL	Liverpool	Old Trafford	W 1–0	–
25.01.06	LC	Blackburn Rovers	Old Trafford	W 2–1	–
29.01.06	FAC	Wolves	Molineux	W 3–0	–
01.02.06	PL	Blackburn Rovers	Ewood Park	L 3–4	–
04.02.06	PL	Fulham	Old Trafford	W 4–2	–
11.02.06	PL	Portsmouth	Fratton Park	W 3–1	–
18.02.06	FAC	Liverpool	Anfield	L 0–1	–
26.02.06	LC	Wigan Athletic	Old Trafford	W 4–0	2
06.03.06	PL	Wigan Athletic	JJB Stadium	W 2–1	–
12.03.06	PL	Newcastle United	Old Trafford	W 2–0	2
18.03.06	PL	West Bromwich Albion	The Hawthorns	W 2–1	–
26.03.06	PL	Birmingham City	Old Trafford	W 3–1	1
29.03.06	PL	West Ham United	Old Trafford	W 1–0	–
01.04.06	PL	Bolton Wanderers	Reebok Stadium	L 1–2	–
09.04.06	PL	Arsenal	Old Trafford	W 2–0	1
14.04.06	PL	Sunderland	Old Trafford	D 0–0	–
17.04.06	PL	Tottenham Hotspur	White Hart Lane	W 2–1	2
29.04.06	PL	Chelsea	Stamford Bridge	L 3–0	–

Total games played = 48
Total goals scored = 15 in League, 3 in Cups
KEY: PL = PREMIER LEAGUE;   LC = LEAGUE CUP;   FAC = FA CUP;
ECLQ = EUROPEAN CHAMPIONS LEAGUE QUALIFIER; ECL = EUROPEAN
CHAMPIONS LEAGUE.

APPENDIX TWO

England Career

For ENGLAND 2003–06

Date	Competition	Opponents	Venue	Result	Rooney Goals
2002–2003 SEASON					
12.02.03	FR	Australia	Upton Park	L 1–3	–
29.03.03	ECQ	Liechtenstein	Vaduz	W 2–0	–
02.04.03	ECQ	Turkey	Stadium of Light	W 2–0	–
03.06.03	FR	Serbia & Montenegro	Walkers Stadium	W 2–1	–
11.06.03	ECQ	Slovakia	Riverside Stadium	W 2–1	–
2003–04 SEASON					
06.09.03	ECQ	Macedonia	Skopje	W 2–1	1
10.09.03	ECQ	Liechtenstein	Old Trafford	W 2–0	1
11.10.03	ECQ	Turkey	Istanbul	D 0–0	–
16.11.03	FR	Denmark	Old Trafford	L 2–3	1
18.02.04	FR	Portugal	Faro	D 1–1	–
31.03.04	FR	Sweden	Gothenburg	L 0–1	–
01.06.04	FR	Japan	City of Manchester	D 1–1	–
05.06.04	FR	Iceland	City of Manchester	W 6–1	2
13.06.04	EC	France	Lisbon	L 1–2	–
17.06.04	EC	Switzerland	Coimbra	W 3–0	2
21.06.04	EC	Croatia	Lisbon	W 4–2	2
24.06.04	EC	Portugal	Lisbon	D 2–2*	–

2004–05 SEASON

09.10.04	WCQ	Wales	Old Trafford	W 2–0	–
13.10.04	WCQ	Azerbaijan	Baku	W 1–0	–
17.11.04	FR	Spain	Bernabeu	W 1–0	–
09.02.05	FR	Holland	Villa Park	D 0–0	–
26.03.05	WCQ	Northern Ireland	Old Trafford	W 4–0	–
30.03.05	WCQ	Azerbaijan	St James' Park	W 2–0	–

2005–06 SEASON

17.08.05	FR	Denmark	Copenhagen	W 4–1	1
03.09.05	WCQ	Wales	Millennium Stadium	W 1–0	–
07.09.05	WCQ	Northern Ireland	Windsor Park	L 0–1	–
12.10.05	WCQ	Poland	Old Trafford	W 2–1	–
12.11.05	FR	Argentina	Geneva	W 3–2	1
01.03.06	FR	Uruguay	Anfield	W 2–1	–
15.06.06	WC	Trinidad & Tobago	Nuremberg	W 1–0	–
20.06.06	WC	Sweden	Cologne	D 2–2	–
25.06.06	WC	Ecuador	Stuttgart	W 1–0	–
01.07.06	WC	Portugal	Gelsenkirchen	D 0–0*	–

Total caps = 33

Total goals scored = 11

KEY: FR = FRIENDLY;   ECQ = EUROPEAN CHAMPIONSHIP QUALIFIER;
EC = EUROPEAN CHAMPIONSHIP FINALS;   WCQ = WORLD CUP QUALIFIER;
WC = WORLD CUP FINALS.

(*Portugal won on penalties)

APPENDIX THREE

Honours

ACHIEVEMENTS

Youngest England International
England v Australia – 12.02.03 (since superseded by Theo
   Walcott, England v Hungary – 30.05.06)

Youngest England International scorer
   Macedonia v England – 06.09.03

Top goalscorer for England at Euro 2004 – 4 goals

Transfer to Manchester United to become the most expensive
   teenager in world football £30 million — 31.08.04

Hat-trick on Manchester United debut v Fenerbahçe –
   28.09.04

AWARDS

BBC Young Sports Personality of the Year 2002

European Player of the Year Nominee 2004

European Golden Boot 2004

FIFA World Player of the Year Nominee 2004

PFA Young Player of the Year 2005

FIFPro Young Player of the Year 2005

FIFA World Player of the Year Nominee 2006

PFA Young Player of the Year 2006

FIFPro Young Player of the Year 2006

The Rooney Report

I always love the questions, surveys and lists in matchday programmes and football magazines, even when sometimes they
are clearly taking the mickey. Here's some true stuff about me,
facts as well as opinions, as of now – but who knows how some
of it might have changed by the time we get to another World
Cup . . .

PERSONAL

Full name: Wayne Mark Rooney.
Born: 24 October 1985, Croxteth, Liverpool.
Parents: Dad (Thomas) Wayne Rooney, labourer; Mum
    Jeanette, dinner lady.
Brothers: Graeme and John.
Secondary education: De La Salle School, left at 16, no
    certificates.
Height: 5ft 10in.
Weight: 12st 10lb.
Fiancée: Coleen McLoughlin, born Croxteth, 3 April 1986.

FAVOURITE THINGS

House: Six-bed detached, with indoor pool, in Cheshire.

Cars: Aston Martin Vanquish 'S', Range Rover, Mercedes SLK.

Newspapers: None – well, only if there's one lying around.

Last holiday: Barbados.

Hobbies, interests: TV, music, films, pool, darts.

TV programmes: Sopranos, Coronation Street, EastEnders, Only Fools and Horses.

TV stars: Lee Evans, Chubby Brown.

Least favourite TV personality: Jonathan Ross.

Music: 50 Cent, Jay-Z, Stereophonics, Arctic Monkeys; also the musical Oliver – I can sing every tune.

Films: One Flew Over the Cuckoo's Nest, Dumb and Dumber, Austin Powers, Stir Crazy.

Actor: Brad Pitt.

Actress: Halle Berry.

Food: Spaghetti Bolognese.

Drink: Sauvignon Blanc white wine.

Sweets: As a child, I loved wine gums, pear drops and bonbons. Now I just have wine gums.

Clothes designer: I'm not really interested in clothes. I tend to go twice a year to a shop in Manchester and buy a load of whatever they have.

The Rooney Report

Last film seen: Cinderella Man.

Last book read: Authorised biography of The Beatles by
Hunter Davies. Well, I've got to page 80. I hop to finish it at
the World Cup . . .

How often do you have a drink?
Once a week, I have about half a bottle of white wine, on a
Saturday or Sunday evening, after a game.

When were you last drunk?
Back in April at Coleen's 20th birthday party. It was at
Lounge Ten, a restaurant in Manchester. I started with a
couple of glasses of Champagne before the meal. That's what
did it . . .

Do you smoke?
No. I did try it when I was 14, but gave up after a few puffs.
On holiday, after a meal, I might have one cigar.

Great hair style. Who cuts it?
Ha, ha. Either Coleen or her mum. I never go to a hairdresser,
can't be bothered. I'm not interested in hairstyles – I either
have mine short, or very short.

When did you first realise you were rich?
About a year ago – when, for the first time, I bought
something without looking at the price label. It was a coat
from a shop called Flannels in Manchester. It cost £5,000.
I regretted it later . . .

Which babe do you fancy most, apart from Coleen?
Beyoncé.

Wayne Rooney: My Story So Far

Which bloke would you most like to look like?
Brad Pitt.

Politics – who do you vote for?
I've never voted. Not interested.

Do you follow current affairs?
No.

Religion?
I'm Roman Catholic. I believe in God, but don't go to church regularly.

Can you cook?
I've only cooked one meal in my life – that was three years ago at our house in Formby, when I was playing for Everton. I made steak and chips with a peppercorn sauce and sweetcorn for me and Coleen. I did it on a George Foreman grill. The ingredients were in the house. While making it, I had to ring Coleen for help. Turned out nice, actually. But I've never cooked another meal; Coleen does it all. She does very good chicken, fish and spag bol.

Do you do any housework?
I have washed the dishes, now and again, but that's all.

If you weren't answering these questions, what would you be doing?
Watching TV.

What phrase do you use most often?
What's happening?

The most surprising thing which has ever happened to you . . .
My first full England call-up. I thought it was for the Under-21s.

The Rooney Report

A common misconception about you is . . .
I'm a scally thug, so the papers seem to think. In real life I'm
very sensitive and very funny. Well, I think so.

If I was Prime Minister, I would . . .
Lock up all traffic wardens.

I'm good at . . .
Driving, so I like to think.

I'm rubbish at . . .
Anything to do with DIY.

In moments of weakness . . .
I'll eat sticky toffee pudding.

In a bad temper I will . . .
Slam the door, ignore people.

What irritates Coleen most about me is . . .
Biting my nails.

What irritates me most about Coleen is . . .
When she grinds her teeth in her sleep. It does my head in, so
I wake her up.

Which three words best describe you?
Romantic, funny, hard.

In what way are you romantic?
For Coleen's 18th birthday I took out an ad in the Liverpool
Echo saying, 'Coleen McLoughlin: My Babe is 18, Happy
Birthday. Love always, Wayne xxx' I am always sending her
flowers, every two weeks or so, even when she's at home.

Tell us a joke then . . .
What do you call an orange crossing the road? Squash. Ha, ha.

Wayne Rooney: My Story So Far

If you hadn't been a footballer, what would you have liked to have been in a fantasy world?
A rock singer.

But what do you think you would have been?
On the dole.

FOOTBALL

What team did you support as a boy?
Everton, of course.

Childhood heroes?
Duncan Ferguson of Everton; Michael Owen, watching him scoring goals for England; and Alan Shearer.

At what age did you think you would make it as a pro player?
I joined Everton's School of Excellence at nine, but it wasn't until I was about 15 that I thought I'd make it.

Greatest influence on your career?
Colin Harvey who was coach of Everton's Under-19s youth teams for two years.

Would you say you have been lucky – or has it been mostly natural ability and hard work?
I would put hard work first, then natural ability – and then luck. I needed luck to break into the Everton team when I did, and then England.

Best goal ever scored?
For Manchester Utd against Newcastle at Old Trafford on 24 April 2005 when we beat them 2–1. One of their defenders had headed out a clearance, and I caught it on the volley from about 25 yards and it flew into the top corner.

The Rooney Report

Just a few seconds before I had been arguing with the ref, can't remember what about now. I wasn't really looking for the ball when it seemed to fall out of the sky. I whacked it out of frustration and anger at the ref – and it flew in. It was voted Goal of the Season on TV.

Best game ever played?
My debut for Manchester Utd on 28 September 2004 when we played Fenerbahçe in the European Champions League. I got a hat-trick.

Best British players played with or against?
Paul Scholes, Stevie Gerrard.

Best Foreign player played with or against?
Zinedine Zidane of France.

Most admired player, past or present?
Diego Maradona of Argentina.

Most admired manager?
Sir Alex Ferguson – and no, not because he's the boss of Manchester Utd, but because he's the best.

Young players to watch?
Cesc Fabregas of Arsenal, Lionel Messi of Barcelona, and Giuseppe Rossi and Gerard Pique of Manchester Utd.

Fave football stadium?
Old Trafford, followed by the Bernabéu in Madrid.

Which TV football commentator and pundit do you most like?
John Motson and Jamie Redknapp.

What would you say are your best qualities?
Shooting, passing.

Wayne Rooney: My Story So Far

And which is your weakest?
Heading.

Do you feel aged 20, 30 or 40?
In ordinary life, I always feel the age I am, 20. When I come
off the pitch I often feel I can't move, so then I feel about 30.

Any pre-match dressing room superstitions?
Not really, apart from the fact that I now tend to put on my
shirt sitting at one place, then my boots and socks elsewhere.

Any nicknames?
In the Manchester Utd dressing room I'm known as Wazza.

What's the best thing about being a pro footballer?
Running out on the pitch at three o'clock.

And the worst?
Press intrusion into your private life.

*Do you get as much fun out of playing football now, aged 20,
with all the pressures, as you did at 15?*
I get more pleasure now. I like playing in front of thousands
of fans and all the games are more competitive.

Has Fergie ever given you the 'hair dryer' treatment?
I'm not sure what that means, but he told me that in one
match I was shite (against Sunderland in April 2006). I have
seen him kick a plastic cup across the dressing room floor, but
not at me.

Is scoring a goal better than sex?
They're both excellent.

Is there too much diving?
Yeah, especially amongst foreigners, and particularly the
Chelsea players. Only half joking . . .

The Rooney Report

What do you think of the standard of refs?
I think too many are trying to be stars.

Do you think modern footballers are overpaid?
Not really. There's a lot of money in football. Why should
players refuse what is on offer?

Who is your preferred striking partner?
At Manchester Utd, I like playing with both Ruud van
Nistelrooy and Louis Saha. They have different strengths.
Ruud holds the ball up so well, and is good at link-up play
and scoring. Louis looks to get behind the defence which gives
me more space. For England, I have only really played up
front with Michael Owen. They are all good players. I don't
have a favourite.

*Has being injured ever worried you that it might ruin your
chances of playing in the World Cup, or your whole career?*
I don't think about getting injured. It has never entered my
mind, even up to the moment when my metatarsal was broken
against Chelsea in April 2006.

*In ten years' time, do you think you'll still be playing for
Manchester Utd?*
Yeah, I hope so.

Would you like to play abroad at some stage in your career?
Don't know. I think my game is best suited to England.

Would you like to stay in football when your career is over?
Don't know. Never thought about it.

Index

301

Index

Index

Index

Index